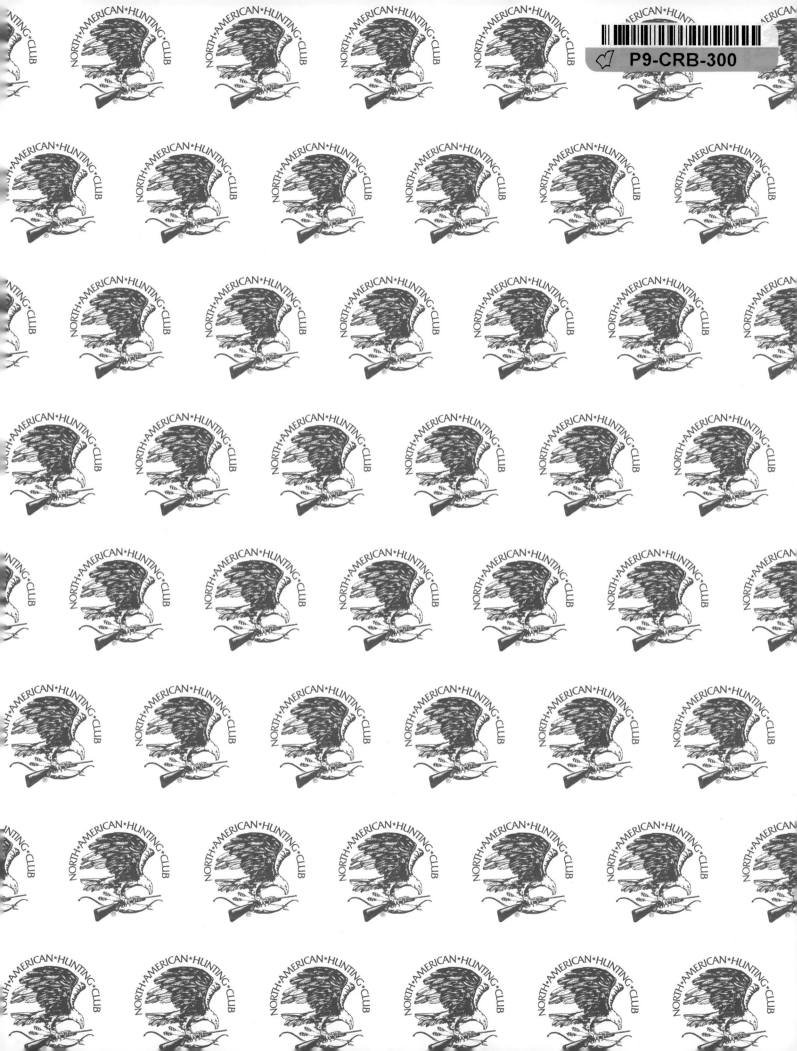

Hunting Black Bears

Hunting Wisdom Library™

MINNETONKA, MINNESOTA

About the Author

*B*ob Robb's articles and photographs have appeared regularly in many major outdoor magazines for nearly two decades. His big game hunting adventures have taken him around the world. Bob began hunting black bears in college; since that time, he has taken black bears on hound, bait, and spot-and-stalk hunts using many different types of firearms, muzzleloaders and handguns. But his favorite way to hunt bears is with bow and arrow. An editor for several national hunting magazines for 15 years, Bob is currently a full-time freelance writer, member of the North American Hunting Club's Bowhunting Advisory Council and an active participant in the fight against the anti-hunting movement.

HUNTING BLACK BEARS

Printed in 2005.

Tom Carpenter
Creative Director

Heather Koshiol
Sr. Book Development Coordinator

Jenya Prosmitsky
Book Design and Production

Dan Kennedy
Photo Editor

Phil Aarrestad
Commissioned Photography

Beowulf, Ltd.
Maps

David Rottinghaus
Illustrations

5 6 7 8 / 08 07 06 05
ISBN 1-58159-137-3
© 2001 North American Hunting Club

North American Hunting Club
12301 Whitewater Drive
Minnetonka, Minnesota 55343
www.huntingclub.com

PHOTO CREDITS

Phil Aarrestad: 22-23, 26, 38 (top), 58 (top left), 58 (top left and bottom), 60, 61 (top), 130-131; **Judd Cooney:** 14 (top), 36, 53, 56, 57, 63 (bottom right), 64 (bottom), 65, 68, 69 (bottom), 71, 81 (bottom), 88-89, 94 (bottom), 96, 107 (top), 107 (bottom right), 109, 111, 121 (bottom), 124 (bottom), 127, 133 (top), 134 (both), 135 (both), 144-145, 151 (bottom), 152, 154, 156-157, 166-167, 173; **Michael Francis:** 158, 169 (bottom); **Don Jones:** 1, 4, 8-9, 13 bottom, 18 (both), 20 (left), 20 (right), 21 (bottom), 24, 32 (left), 45 (both), 46, 48-49, 49 (top), 54 (top), 62 (left), 72-73, 75 (both), 76, 77 (bottom), 83, 84 (top), 86, 87 (bottom), 98-99, 102 (bottom), 107 (bottom left), 108 (top), 118-119, 129 (bottom), 169 (top), 170 (both), 171; **Rich Kirchner/The Green Agency:** 17 (top), 126 (right), 164, 168; **Lee Kline:** 12 (top left), 47, 49 (bottom), 54 (bottom), 59 (right), 66, 101, 81 (top), 123, 132; **Tony Knight:** 37 (top); **Gordy Krahn/Krause Publishing:** 110; **Bill Lea:** Cover, 10, 160 (both); **Rob Nye/The Green Agency:** 115, 125 (top); **Mark Raycroft:** 6-7, 10, 12 (top right), 18 (top), 19, 78 (bottom), 80 (top), 94 (top), 105, 120, 124 (top), 125 (middle), 125 (bottom), 126 (left); **Bob Robb:** 12 (bottom left), 21 (top), 25, 30, 31 (bottom), 34 (bottom right), 40, 41, 42 (top), 44, 59 (left), 63 (bottom left), 69 (top), 70, 77 (top), 79, 85, 91 (bottom), 100, 103 (top), 104, 106 (bottom), 116 (top), 138, 139, 140 (top); **Jim Shockey:** 58 (top right); **Dusan Smetana/The Green Agency:** 161; **Richard Smith:** 90, 91 (top), 92, 93, 95, 117 (top); **Ron Spomer:** 117 (bottom); **Tom Teitz:** 82; **Bryce Towsley:** 27, 28; **Bill Vaznis/The Green Agency:** 74, 112-113, 114, 146, 151 (top), 152 (bottom), 153; **Larry Weishun:** 42 (bottom); **Mark Werner:** 11 (both), 12 (bottom right), 13 (top), 14 (bottom), 15, 16 (both), 17 (bottom), 31 (top), 50-51, 52, 55, 61 (bottom), 63 (top), 67 (bottom), 78 (top), 80 (bottom), 103 (bottom), 106 (top), 108 (bottom), 116 (bottom), 149, 159, 162, 165, 172. **Remaining images property of NAHC:** 32 (right), 33 (both), 34 (left), 34 (top right), 35 (both), 37 (bottom), 38 (bottom), 39, 62 (right), 67 (top left), 67 (top right), 84 (bottom), 87 (top), 97, 133 (bottom), 136, 137, 141, 142, 147 (both), 148, 150.

Table of Contents

Foreword

You need only be close to a black bear once and you'll know exactly what I mean. You're on your stand, whether hunting bears or deer or some other game, and it's a perfectly normal day. Birds are singing. Squirrels chase through the leaves. Perhaps a grouse or a flock of turkeys feeds nearby.

Suddenly the woods become absolutely silent. The birds and squirrels are gone. There isn't a puff of breeze. The hairs on your neck are standing on end.

Next you catch the sound of a deadfall branch breaking just beyond the wall of spruce upwind of your stand. Then silence again.

You look back to the bait or game trail in front of you, and there's a black bear! You never heard it; you never saw it approach. It's as if it materialized on the spot. How can an animal that big and lumbering be that quiet?

Sometimes a bear will come charging into a bait or make all kinds of noise and threatening gestures as it moves through the woods. But most times bears appear suddenly, silently ... almost out of thin air. It's the way of a predator.

How do the birds know to stop singing and the squirrels to hide in their nests? What causes the hair on the neck of even the first-time hunter to stand on end *before* he knows there's a bear around? Those of us who have hunted black bears know—it's simply the difference between hunting prey like deer and hunting a predator at the top of the food chain!

Most of the U.S. today is blessed with a growing black bear population. Hunting is opening up in locales that haven't had bear seasons in 50 years or more! That's creating wonderful opportunity for NAHC members to sample the exciting challenge of hunting black bears virtually in their own back yards.

Because the habitat of the black bear is so varied, and because the population is spreading, there's also a wide variety of techniques and methods for NAHC members to attempt. Baiting, hound hunting, driving, stand hunting, glass-and-stalk and even calling are all viable, ethical, legal hunting methods practiced in the U.S. and Canada today. Best of all, they all offer good chances of success if undertaken knowledgeably and skillfully.

That's where Bob Robb and this book come into play. There's nobody better than lifelong black bear hunter and writer Bob Robb to help you hone your black bear hunting skills no matter which method or hunting tool you employ.

Let's follow Bob into bear country ... and bring your steadiest nerves.

Best afield,

Bill

Bill Miller
Executive Director, North American Hunting Club

INTRODUCTION

*I*t had been a grand spring bear season. I had spent several days preparing two different bait sites, then monitoring the resulting activity. In addition, I had spent several days and evenings after work glassing bears on the steep mountains near my home. I had climbed long and hard in pursuit of a couple of dandy boars, to no avail. Both baits had hosted lots of activity, though mostly from sows and cubs, or immature boars. But I saw bears every evening I sat a bait. I would shoot some pictures and video footage and generally enjoy the time. Why stay home and watch TV when you can watch black bears, up close and personal?

Then late one evening, a big boar came to my bait. He was a bruiser with a perfect jet-black coat that shimmered in the shadows when he strutted in. My broadhead found its mark, and the tracking job was a short one. It was after midnight as I sat and held his head, stroked his thick coat and thought deeply about how lucky I was to live—and hunt—in an area filled with *Ursus americanus*, the black bear.

Black bear hunting is something few big game hunters ever experience on their own. Most who choose to hunt bears do it but once, and then only with the aid of a guide or outfitter. Once they have their bear rug and skull, that's the end of it. And while I am a big fan of quality guided hunting, that typical experience is kind of a shame. These folks do not spend enough time in the bear woods to appreciate what a magnificent animal the black bear is.

Black bears are one of North America's most misunderstood big game animals. Thanks to media-created impressions, many see bears as big buffoons, playful and carefree, the friend of man. In truth, they are secretive in nature, possessing tremendous physical strength and speed. On rare occasions, they can be extremely dangerous. Fatal black bear attacks on humans occur annually.

Every time I head into the bear woods, I learn something new about the bears and about myself. With bear numbers growing across the animal's range, there has never been a better opportunity for you to experience the excitement of hunting one of the continent's most interesting big game animals.

Want to learn more? Then come along as we explore the world of black bear hunting. You'll be glad you did.

—Bob Robb

Chapter 1

ALL ABOUT
BLACK BEARS

Few animals inspire outdoorsmen and women more than bears do. These large, powerful animals have been living in North America for eons, yet they remain largely misunderstood even by those who spend an inordinate amount of time in the woods.

What do bears eat? Are they dangerous? Do they really sleep all winter? How many cubs do they have, and how big are they at birth? Are bears fast? Do they see as poorly as most people believe? How about that sense of smell? Can bears hear me coming? Are they clumsy or deft? Fast or slow? Smart or dumb?

Just as modern hunters do, the Native Americans and, later, white settlers, lived with and hunted black bears for meat and hides, and as trophies to be displayed proudly. In the early days, bear populations were so high that it did not take a trained biologist's knowledge of their habits and haunts to regularly kill them. In some areas—notably large, unsettled portions of Alaska and Canada—this is still true to some degree. There are just so many bears that finding one isn't all that difficult.

Across the rest of their range, though, finding a mature black bear to hunt can be much more difficult than locating a mature bull elk or buck deer. There aren't as many bears, their secretive nature keeps them away from people, and their habit of moving constantly in search of food makes patterning them tough. Today's black bear hunters need to be armed with all the information they can process regarding the biology of the black bear.

Come along with us then, and enter the world of the black bear. The more you know, the better your chances for a successful bear hunt and for enjoyment of the natural world in which these wonderful animals live.

Black bears symbolize all that is wild and good. They are handsome, smart, cagey, shy, bold, big ... and so much more.

Hunting Black Bears

BLACK BEAR BIOLOGY

The black bear (*Ursus americanus americanus*) is a uniquely North American animal. Found all across Alaska and Canada, in 32 U.S. states and in the most northerly reaches of Old Mexico, black bears have been found in North America since prehistoric times.

While the vast majority of bears live in the north, good populations can be found on the East Coast south through the Appalachian Mountains, and in the Southeast from Florida across to southern Louisiana. In the West they can be found from Washington down through southern California and over into southern Arizona.

Black bear populations are also increasing in many areas of the United States, often in places where they had previously not been viewed as a "problem" by local residents. Not a day goes by without a news account of bears in someone's backyard, either in mid-Atlantic states like Maryland, New Jersey and New York, or in Western states like California, Oregon and Washington. And around many prominent national parks, bears often break into campers' cars in search of food. Even in Florida, where bears have been protected for several years because of low populations, nuisance bear complaints have recently risen so dramatically that state officials have considered reopening limited hunting.

TAXONOMY

Most mature black bear boars (males) stand 3 to $3^{1}/_{2}$ feet high at the shoulder and are 4 to $6^{1}/_{2}$ feet long. Sows (females) are perhaps two-thirds the size of comparable boars. Black bears can grow quite large, depending on where they live and what they eat.

On average, mature boars weigh between 200 and 300 pounds across most of their range, with sows weighing between 150 and 250 pounds. But much larger bears have been recorded. Along the coast of British Columbia and Alaska, specimens weighing upwards of 400 pounds are not uncommon. I know of bears from both California and the Carolinas that have weighed upwards of 800 pounds. For example, Tennessee resident Coy

Mature boars stand 3 to $3^{1}/_{2}$ feet high at the shoulder, are 4 to $6^{1}/_{2}$ feet long, and average between 200 and 300 pounds. Boars that live in areas of "easy living," with consistently good food sources, can weigh much more.

On average, sows are about two-thirds the size of boars and have what appears to be a longish, pointed snout. Mature boars have a more short, squarish "stovepipe" nose.

Black bear eyes are a deep, dark brown color, and smaller compared to other predators'. Though good, a bear's eyesight is its weakest sense.

A bear's rounded ears—which measure between 4$\frac{1}{2}$ and 6 inches long—allow him or her to hear very well. The black bear's sense of smell rivals any game animal on the continent.

Parton killed an 880-pound black bear in Craven County, North Carolina. An 827-pounder was taken in Pennsylvania some years ago.

Black bears have five relatively short, curved claws on each foot, designed to help them dig up food and to facilitate tree climbing. Front claws are much longer than rear claws. Black bear eyes are dark brown, and are small in comparison to other predators'. Their eyesight is their weakest sense, though not as weak as many people believe. It has been determined that bears can see some colors, and they can spot movement incredibly well.

A bear's ears are rounded, and measure 4$\frac{1}{2}$ to 6 inches long, allowing them to hear very well. Their sense of smell is superb, equal to that of any

big game animal on the continent. Black bears also have short, stubby tails between 3 and 5 inches long, but because they keep them clamped down tightly against the rump it is hard to see them.

Though they have relatively short legs, black bears can move quite rapidly over steep, broken terrain. Black bears have been clocked as fast as 33 mph—much faster than a man can run. They can also climb the steepest mountains and even cliffs (which they readily do), and deftly walk across narrow fallen logs spanning deep canyons and swift rivers. Superb swimmers, black bears spend lots of time in and around water, especially in hot weather.

Black bears are heavily muscled, with massive front shoulders, huge rumps, thick legs and large

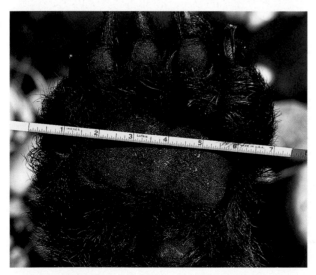

A large black bear's paw is a fearsome thing, with short claws and a thick pad. Measuring across the pad is a good indicator of a bear's size.

Excellent swimmers, black bears spend a lot of time in and around water, especially in summer when temperatures in black bear country soar.

necks. They are extremely strong and lightning quick. Their hair is lush and thick, an excellent insulator in cold weather. As the bears emerge from their dens in spring and the weather warms, they tend to rub off large portions of their hair. It grows back quickly, and by the time they are ready to den up for winter, they have plenty of warm hair again.

LIFE SPAN & BREEDING

Black bears can live longer than most people realize. Ages between 20 and 30 years have been recorded on both wild and captive bears. The oldest black bear I have ever heard of was a male shot by a hunter in New York State in 1974 that was aged at $41^{1}/_{2}$ years. Bears are aged by looking at a small premolar tooth that is cross-sectioned and studied under a microscope. The inside of a bear's

Young black bear cubs are quite playful, chasing each other and wrestling a lot like kittens. They are amazingly nimble at a very early age.

Bears breed in May and early June. On average, a sow will have a litter of 2 or 3 cubs every two years, with cubs usually born in the den in January or early February. Despite the large size they reach at adulthood, cubs usually weigh only about 12 ounces at birth. They are born hairless with their eyes closed.

This bear found shelter for the winter under a rock ledge.

Black bears use a variety of sites for dens, including rock caves, hollow logs, old beaver lodges, culverts, and sheltered areas under uprooted trees and brush piles. The time spent in the den varies by region. Bears in more northerly, cold climates with harsher winters spend more time in the den than bears in more temperate, southerly locations. In some areas at the southern apex of their range, such as Florida, Arizona and southern California, the bears might not den up for any appreciable amount of time at all.

A black bear's normal body temperature is about 100° to 101°F. While a bear is in its den, its body temperature may drop to as low as 88°. A bear's heart rate during deep hibernation might slow to just 10 beats a minute, and breathing slows to one breath every 45 seconds. Because of this slowing of body functions, bears do not have to eliminate waste as they do when they are awake. Though they may not urinate, they may defecate on occasion during hibernation. After hibernation, bears normally pass large quantities of fecal matter.

Bears do not necessarily remain asleep during the entire denning period, even in the most northerly climates. Many times, I have seen bear tracks on Alaska snow fields in the dead of winter. Reports of bears spotted roaming in winter are rare, but not so rare as to be considered extremely unusual.

teeth have growth rings, just as trees do, with each ring representing a year of life.

Bears typically mate from late May through early June, though they can breed into summer. A sow has a litter of two or three cubs (but occasionally as few as one or as many as five) every two years. A sow can mate in her third year of life, usually producing a single cub that first year, then two or three in subsequent breeding years. Males can breed beginning at $2^{1}/_{2}$ years of age and are quite polygamous. When a male runs across a sow in heat, he will often trail her much the way a white-tailed buck trails a doe.

Most cubs are born in January or early February, though they may be born in late December or early March. Despite reaching such a large, muscular size, it is interesting to note that cubs, at birth, weigh only about 12 ounces. The cubs are nearly hairless and their eyes are closed at birth. The eyes are usually open by 6 weeks of age. While nursing cubs, sows can lose up to a third of their body weight.

BEAR DENS & HIBERNATION

Pennsylvania biologist Gary Alt measured several bear dens, noting that they are smaller than most people believe. Of 400 dens Alt measured, the average den covered just 19 cubic feet, with a typical entrance measuring 17 inches wide and 19 inches tall, and an interior measuring about $5^{1}/_{2}$ feet long, 32 inches wide and 23 inches tall.

This bear chose to spend the winter hunkered under the base of an up-rooted tree.

HABITAT & HOME RANGE

Black bear habitat encompasses a wide variety of places, depending on the region in which the animals live. Out West, bears generally live in forests and wooded mountains from sea level to roughly 7,500 feet elevation. In the East, wooded mountains, flatland forests and swamps are the primary habitat. Bears tend to prefer thick cover to wide-open spaces.

A black bear's home range can vary widely, from relatively small to quite large. Pennsylvania biologist Gary Alt's studies show that in Pennsylvania, males have a home range of between 60 and 75 square miles, with this range area measuring 5 to 15 miles across at its widest point. A female's much smaller home range averages 12 to 15 square miles and 3 to 5 miles across. These home range sizes seem to be representative of the largest ranges across the continent.

On the other hand, the smallest range I have heard of was on Long Island in Washington's Willapa National Wildlife Refuge. It measured 2 square miles and just .8 mile across. In the Great Smoky Mountains National Park, males had a home range average of 4.2 square miles, sows 2.6

Although it's not common, some black bears do get out for winter forays.

The size of a black bear's home territory can vary widely, depending on where he lives. Black bears are sometimes quite possessive of this home range.

square miles. Boars roam most often during the rut, when they are actively seeking estrus sows.

Black bears are sometimes quite possessive of their home territory. This is clear when biologists attempt to trap and move "problem" bears out of a troubled area and into a new home range. It almost cannot be done, with most of these bears returning rapidly over distances of 100 miles or more to their original home range, often ending up right back at the same garbage dump! I know of several instances where problem bears were flown from a mainland garbage dump to an island many miles offshore, only to return to the same dump in less than a few weeks.

Biologists still do not know how bears find their way home, just that they do it so often that today, problem bears are usually destroyed to avoid an expensive and generally futile trapping and transporting exercise.

Bears are most active after dark. Studies have shown that, at least during hunting seasons, more bears are seen from late afternoon until dark than at any other time period. Dawn to early morning is the second most active period. Except during breeding season or when congregating to eat at dumps or on fish streams, bears live a solitary life.

WHAT DO BLACK BEARS EAT?

Black bears are omnivores, eating both meat and plants, with flora making up the bulk of their diet. Stomach content analyses done by biologists have shown that about 86 percent of a bear's diet consists of plants. They will eat just about anything—from twigs, buds, leaves, nuts, roots, fruit, corn and berries to newly sprouted plants, especially grasses, on which they graze like cattle or elk. In spring, bears will peel bark from trees to get at the cambium. They will destroy rotted logs to get at bugs, beetles, crickets and ants inside, and they love to eat larvae. Honey is nectar to bears. When available, they gorge on fish, especially where there are runs of anadromous fishes, as there are in Alaska, British Columbia and the West Coast states.

In each region, bears have certain plants they prefer over others. For example, in areas of Oregon, they love manzanita berries. In the fall,

Black bears are omnivores, eating everything from plants to meat. Newly sprouted leaves are consumed when available.

In coastal areas, black bears become quite accomplished fishermen, gorging themselves on migrating salmon in late spring and summer. These coastal bears can grow quite large thanks to this protein-rich diet.

in many western mountain states, berries such as huckleberries, blackberries and blueberries are preferred. Arizona bears love prickly pear cactus, among other things. In Minnesota and other parts of the upper Midwest, grasses, mushrooms, catkins, aspen leaves and fruits and berries are staples. In late summer and early fall, dogwood berries, hazelnuts, wild cherries, mountain ash, apples and their favorite, acorns, are preferred. In the Northeast, beechnuts are a favorite food. Wherever corn is planted, bears will be in it, big time. The same is true of other crops, notably oats, soybeans and wheat.

Bears will also opportunistically feed on small animals, catching and eating what they can. Squirrels, rabbits, hares, rodents, frogs, birds and bird's eggs, beavers and so on are all caught and eaten, as are trout, suckers, salmon and other easily caught fishes when they are available. Bears will also chase and catch small ungulates, including deer fawns, as well as caribou, moose and elk calves. They are very efficient at catching these young animals, but rarely attempt to take down an adult.

Black bears are opportunistic feeders, and a fawn is a good opportunity for a bear.

Are All Black Bears Black?

While black is the predominant color of black bears, there are variations. These variations tend to be geographical, though it is certainly possible for a "color phase" bear to turn up throughout the range.

Most black bears are jet-black with brown muzzles. Some of these jet-black bears have white markings on their chest, little more than spots on some bears and a prominent V-shape on others.

The most common off-black color phase is a light brown or cinnamon color. Cinnamon bears are found predominately in certain areas of the West but they have been taken across Canada and as far east as Pennsylvania in the Lower 48.

The most common off-black color phase of black bears is a cinnamon, or light brown, color.

Brown-phase bears are a regional phenomenon. For example, one study conducted in Washington State showed that Olympic Peninsula bears were virtually 100 percent black, while more than three-fourths were black along the Skookumchuck, Newaukum, Toutle and Green rivers, with the rest brown-phase bears. Where I often hunt in Prince William Sound, Alaska, virtually all the bears along the coast are black. Move inland 25 miles over the high mountains to the Copper River drainage, and you'll see a high percentage of cinnamon bears.

It is interesting to note that bears born brown as cubs may not stay that way all their lives, but will likely turn into jet-black bears as they age. Other brown-color phases include blond, reddish brown and dark chocolate brown. Though rare, some color-phase bears also have the white chest markings.

Glacier, or blue, black bears have been classified as a separate subspecies. They are found only in the coastal area of southeast Alaska and British Columbia. They are actively hunted in Alaska, but are hard to come by. Glacier bears are jet-black, but have light-colored guard hairs that appear to take on an almost ghost-like blue quality when hit just right by sunlight. The Kermode bear, found only along the British Columbia coast primarily on Grinnell and Princess Royal islands, is a white color phase. They are fully protected. True albino bears are quite rare, but do appear on occasion.

Some black bears are a deep chocolate brown, a color phase that seems to be a regional phenomenon.

Quite rare, a blond black bear is a beautiful anomaly to be admired and treasured.

BEAR SIGN

*I*t is important to know what kinds of sign to look for when scouting for black bears and for places offering good chances at a successful bear hunt. You can generally classify bear sign into groups: feeding sign, bear trees, trails, tracks and scat.

FEEDING SIGN

Sign of bears recently feeding in an area are often easy to recognize. You'll see overturned logs, rocks and even "cow patties." Bears often tear apart rotten stumps and logs in search of insects and grubs. Bears leave distinguishable sign where

they have dug up roots, and also where they have dug up anthills or burrowing rodents.

Trees often show sign of bear abuse. Fruit and nut trees sometimes have branches torn clean off: Rather than climb the tree to eat the fruit, the bears simply tear the limb off and eat at their leisure on the ground. In the fall, if you find that bears have recently ripped limbs off trees—evident by the still-green leaves attached—and there is still edible fruit available, you can be reasonably sure the bear will return. Sometimes, though, the sign of feeding bears in fruit and nut trees is nothing more than claw marks on the trunk. Where they are feeding heavily on berries, you can find berry

When seeking food, black bears often dig up the ground, dig into old logs, flip over old cow patties, and do whatever it takes to find grubs, insects and roots to help satisfy their seemingly insatiable appetites.

bushes ripped apart.

In areas where salmon run up rivers in late summer and fall, you can see evidence of bears feeding on fish by the carcasses left on the bank. Of course, if grizzlies also inhabit the area, one must take care that such fish feeding is not being done by these dangerous bears.

BEAR TREES

Trees scarred with both claw and bite marks can be found in feeding areas and along established trails and travel corridors. Bears also use trees for rubbing, and long-barked trees can retain small bits of bear hair, another sign of recent bear activity.

You can also find evidence that sows have run cubs up trees along travel corridors. Again, claw marks running up and down the trunk are the giveaway signs.

TRAILS

In areas where bear populations have remained strong for generations, it is not uncommon to find well-worn bear trails on the ground. These can be found in low-lying areas. I have seen most

In areas of high bear numbers it is not unusual to find well-worn "bear trails" that the bruins have traveled for centuries.

of these trails on ridges and in tundra areas in the Pacific Northwest, Alaska and Canada. In some areas, the bears instead have used the exact same footprints as those left by other bears that traveled who knows how many hundreds of years before. It is a sobering and wonderful sight.

TRACKS

Black bear tracks are very distinctive, yet can be difficult to locate unless there is sand, mud or another soft surface to hold their impression. Whenever I find an area that holds the kind of foods a bear might like, I search diligently in soft soil, along creek banks and in other areas that might hold a bear track.

The track consists of the impression of the foot pad and toes. Except in very soft, moist soil or mud, you may not see claw marks, though they are worth looking for. Claw marks are one of the ways to quickly tell the difference between black and grizzly bears. Grizzlies almost always leave the marks of their longer claws with their tracks.

Black bear tracks show pads that are longer than they are wide, with the front pads wider and shorter than those of the rear foot. It is possible to closely judge the approximate size of an adult bear

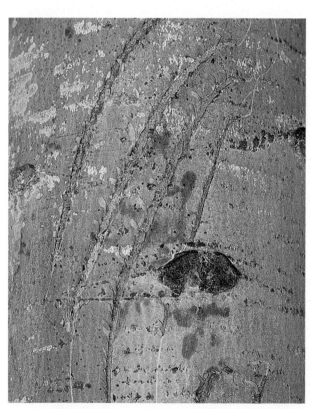

Claw marks are proof positive that a bear has been in the area.

Black bear tracks are very distinctive and are easiest to locate in areas of mud, soft sand or other soft surfaces. Look for both the pad and the toes. Mature boars leave larger tracks than sows.

by measuring across the pad of a front foot track. Simply measure the width of the pad, add one, and you'll have the approximate squared measurement of the bear's hide. (See Chapter 8 for details on how to square a bear hide.) Thus, a pad measuring $4^1/2$ inches across will be made by a black bear with a hide that will square at approximately $5^1/2$ feet.

Boars leave larger tracks than sows. It is rare to find a sow with feet large enough to leave a track more than 4 to $4^1/2$ inches wide. Mature boars, however, will have front pads 5 inches wide or more. The largest track I have personally measured was nearly 7 inches across, and came from a bear I arrowed in southeast Alaska that squared 7 feet 6 inches.

SCAT

Bear scat cannot be confused with that of any other animal in the woods. It is usually a pile of solid, cylindrical chunks filled with roughage from whatever the bear has been eating. In fact, a good way to determine where to hunt bears is to study the scat. If it is full of blueberries, for example, hunting the nearest berry patch makes lots of sense. Bears that have been eating lots of berries

may deposit more of a loose, "cow patty" type of scat.

In areas where bears are feeding heavily or bedding, there will be several piles of fresh and semi-fresh scat. While there are no hard-and-fast rules along these lines, the rule of thumb is this: The larger the scat, the larger the bear.

Very distinctive, bear scat is usually a pile of cylindrical chunks filled with roughage. But bears eating a preponderance of berries may leave more of a cow pie-like dropping.

Chapter 2

BEAR MEDICINE

*T*he young hunter was nervous to begin with. He just knew his .270 wasn't enough gun for the job. His dad had brought him along on a mule deer hunt, purchasing the boy a black bear tag just in case they stumbled on a bear during the week. As luck would have it, that first afternoon found them within 75 yards of a beautiful jet-black boar as he fed in a large mountainside blueberry patch.

The closer they got, the more nervous the young sportsman became. The hunters stopped at 75 yards, got into the prone position, and prepared to shoot. His father was great, calmly telling the boy to take his time, wait for the bear to turn broadside, then shoot him right in the chest. That the boy had spent some time at the rifle range was evident when the 130-grain Speer Spitzer from his .270 took out both lungs. The celebration lasted into the night.

Physically, black bears are incredible animals. They are big, fast and powerful, with thick, heavy muscles, leg bones like steel pipes and shoulder blades like battle shields. There are stories of bears that have been hit poorly and never recovered by the hunter. Those stories, added to tales of bear attacks, make many novice black bear hunters feel sorely under-gunned without some sort of light cannon.

In truth, black bears are not all that difficult to kill cleanly. And of course, no one wants to head into the thick stuff after a poorly hit black bear. Coupled with proper shot placement, choosing a weapon intelligently is the key to success. That's true regardless of the type of weapon you choose, be it rifle, muzzleloader, handgun or bow-and-arrow.

Still, not all bears are created equal. The larger bears more common to some areas should be hunted with a little more "pop" than is used for hunting smaller bears found in other regions. There are also some commonsense guidelines to follow when selecting either a firearm or bow for black bear hunting. Want to know what these guidelines are? Then turn the page …

GUNS & LOADS FOR BLACK BEARS

I remember the first time I went black bear hunting. I had heard all the stories about bears and bear attacks, about how black bears were these giant rough-and-tumble animals that can take your best shot and keep coming. Being young and inexperienced, as well as somewhat lacking in funds, I had few rifles from which to choose and no option for buying a new one. So I brought

There are a wide selection of adequate rifles and cartridges for black bear hunting, and final selection should be based both on the size of bears expected to be encountered and the method of hunting to be employed. Regardless, precise shot placement is critical.

along a battered old pre-64 Winchester Model 70 in .30-06, stuffed with some handloads featuring the 180-grain Nosler Partition bullet. It proved to be a wise decision.

I was on a spot-and-stalk hunt in western Montana, a trip on which I saw far more elk and mule deer than I did bears. When I finally got my chance, I shot a medium-sized bear (about a 200-pounder) at 150 yards. He didn't go 75 yards before piling up.

Since that time, I have seen something in the neighborhood of half-a-hundred black bears taken with firearms of all shapes, sizes and descriptions. The two largest calibers I've seen used are the .375 H&H Mag.—not an uncommon caliber in Alaska or British Columbia when on a combination brown bear/black bear hunt—and .338/.378 Wthby Mag., an incredibly powerful, flat-shooting cartridge suitable for hunting big game animals the size of small automobiles. The smallest caliber I've seen used is the .243 Win., used by a Rocky Mountain deer hunter who happened to have a bear tag in his pocket when we glassed up a bear one crisp fall afternoon.

After all that, I've come to believe that black bears are not indestructible tanks that can take shot after shot and keep going. Certainly there are tougher big game animals out there. But bears are bears, and a poorly hit bear that escapes into thick cover and must be tracked can be bad news. It is a scenario to be avoided.

MATCH THE CARTRIDGE TO THE HUNT

Generally speaking, black bears can be cleanly taken with most standard deer-hunting cartridges. The prudent hunter will make a final cartridge choice based on the specific hunt. Considerations include the type of hunt, the terrain and the size of the bears expected to be encountered.

As we've seen, all black bears are not created equal. The average bear taken on many central Canadian bait hunts weighs maybe 150 pounds. That bear is nothing like the 300- to 450-pound tanks taken on the Alaska and British Columbia coast, or the huge-bodied bears found in more southerly states like California and North Carolina, where 800-pound bears have been weighed on certified scales. Bigger bodies are harder to bring down and require larger bullets and more kinetic energy.

Bears hunted on spot-and-stalk hunts or from

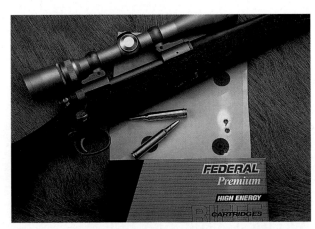

In many areas, bear hunting occurs under wet conditions, making synthetic stocks and stainless steel metalwork an excellent choice.

While there are myriad effective cartridges for black bear hunting, the absolute minimum should be some sort of .25 caliber. I prefer .30 caliber and up because of the larger wound channels these bullets create. Cartridges between the .308 and various .300 magnums are superb choices.

treestands and ground blinds overlooking large cornfields should be hunted with flat-shooting cartridges that permit precise bullet placement at extended distances. This is especially true in areas where the escape cover is as thick as a coastal fog.

On the other hand, where shots will be short—this includes most bait hunts and when following hounds, where shots will probably be less than 30 yards—it makes more sense to use a medium-velocity cartridge featuring a large-caliber bullet with a wide frontal section that makes a big hole.

SPECIFIC CARTRIDGE CHOICES

Regardless of the size of the bears being hunted, in my mind the minimum cartridge should be some sort of .25 caliber, like the .25-06 or .257 Wthby Mag., using bullets weighing between 117 and 120 grains. Cartridges in the .270/.30-06/7mm Mag. class are better, and excellent for black bear hunting coast to coast.

But I personally prefer .30 caliber and up because of the larger wound channels these rounds create. These include the .308, .30-06, and the various .300 magnums. There's really no reason to use more powerful cartridges such as the .338 Win. Mag., .340 Wthby Mag. and the like, unless you simply want to.

Perhaps the best overall black bear cartridges I have used are considered "tame" by some experts. These are .348 and .358 caliber cartridges like the .348 Win., .358 Win. and .35 Whelen, rounds that use relatively heavy bullets with a large frontal section traveling at medium velocity. At the distances most bears are taken—200 yards and less—this combination produces a wallop that really gets their attention and creates a big hole that facilitates blood trailing.

One of the most knowledgeable ballisticians around, and an extremely experienced big game hunter, is my friend Col. Craig Boddington, USMCR. He has an old lever gun in .348 Win. with a classic peep sight that he absolutely loves to take bear hunting. He has proven its effectiveness many times over.

On hunts when you have to move quickly and shoot at close-range targets—hound hunts come immediately to mind—a light rifle that's easy to carry makes sense. Many rifle hunters choose light lever-action rifles chambered for classic cartridges like the .30-30, .300 Sav., .348 Win. and .358 Win. These rifle/cartridge combinations are also excellent choices for most bait hunts.

RIFLE ACTION TYPES

All rifle action types are suitable for black bear hunting. It is more important to use a rifle you are both familiar and comfortable with rather than picking up a new rifle just for the action.

Bolt-action rifles are far and away the most popular in North America for all big game hunting. On hunts when shots might be long, bolt actions are highly accurate, extremely reliable and

All rifle action types are suitable for black bear hunting. While bolt-action rifles are the most popular across the continent, single shots, pump actions, semi-autos, and lever actions (pictured top to bottom) are also very good choices.

offer a relatively quick follow-up shot. Single-shots are also good choices for open-country hunting. Deer hunters who have a pet pump action or autoloader in .30-06, .308, and the like, need look no further when planning a bear hunt.

And lever-action rifles will get it done too. In fact, my own "pet" black bear rifle is a Browning BLR lever-action rifle chambered for the .358 Win. cartridge. When loaded with bullets weighing between 200 and 250 grains, this rifle is highly accurate out to 250 yards, and really lays it on them. I've used it on dog hunts, over bait and on some spot-and-stalk hunts, all with great results.

What About Bullets?

Regardless of the type of bear hunt I am on, I always use stout bullets. "Premium" bullets like the Nosler Partition and Partition Gold, Barnes X-Bullet, Winchester Fail Safe, Speer Grand Slam, Swift A-Frame, and others of similar ilk, are designed for both controlled expansion and deep penetration.

Black bears have thick, dense muscles on their shoulders, backs and legs. These sturdy bullets are designed for maximum penetration while retaining a high percentage of their original weight—a superb combination for a bear's physique as well as for shot angles that are less than ideal. The last thing you want is to use a "soft" bullet that expands too quickly, fragmenting on the hide or just inside the shoulder muscles before getting inside the boiler room. And if you have to take a follow-up shot at the south end of a northbound bear, you'll really appreciate the deep-penetrating design of premium bullets.

I also like some of the "classic" bullets designed for deer and elk hunting. These include Winchester Power Point, Remington Core-Lokt, Federal Hi-Shok, Speer Spitzer, Hornady Interlock, and others in this class. These bullets penetrate well, expand rapidly and retain a good amount of their original weight.

Bullets to avoid are those designed for extremely rapid expansion on smaller, light-skinned animals like pronghorn and small deer. The Nosler Ballistic Tip and Sierra Boattail are two that come immediately to mind. Both are superbly accurate bullets that really knock the heck out of light game, but expand much too rapidly and violently for bears.

Shot Placement Is Key

Keep in mind that, as in all big game hunting, shot placement is much more critical to your success than the caliber rifle you're using. It is far better to go bear hunting with a rifle/cartridge combination with which you are familiar, and that you shoot well, than to go out and buy a new rifle in a larger caliber that you end up being scared of and that you hesitate to practice with. We'll discuss specific shot placement at the end of this chapter.

Regardless of the bear hunt you undertake, using a "premium"-type bullet designed for controlled expansion and deep penetration is a good idea. These bullets will penetrate the heaviest muscle and reach the vital heart/lung area when others may not. Pictured (left to right): Combined Technologies Fail Safe, Combined Technologies Partition Gold Rifle, Nosler Partition, Swift A-Frame, Nosler Ballistic Tip and Barnes X-Bullet.

Select Black Bear Cartridges
CENTERFIRE RIFLES

Cartridge Name	Bullet Weight (grains)	Velocity (fps)					Kinetic Energy (foot-pounds)				
		Muzzle	100 yards	200 yards	300 yards	400 yards	Muzzle	100 yards	200 yards	300 yards	400 yards
.260 Rem.	140	2,750	2,540	2,340	2,150	1,970	2,350	2,010	1,705	1,440	1,210
.270	150	2,850	2,504	2,183	1,886	1,618	2,705	2,087	1,587	1,185	872
.280 Rem.	150	2,890	2,624	2,373	2,135	1,912	2,781	2,293	1,875	1,518	1,217
.280 Rem.	160	2,840	2,637	2,442	2,256	2,078	2,866	2,471	2,120	1,809	1,535
7X57	175	2,440	2,140	1,860	1,600	1,380	2,315	1,775	1,340	1,000	740
7mm-08	140	2,800	2,523	2,268	2,027	1,802	2,429	1,980	1,599	1,277	1,010
7mm Rem. Mag.	160	2,950	2,745	2,550	2,363	2,184	3,093	2,679	2,311	1,984	1,694
7mm Rem. Mag.	175	2,860	2,645	2,440	2,244	2,057	3,178	2,718	2,313	1,956	1,644
.30-30	170	2,200	1,900	1,620	1,380	1,190	1,830	1,355	990	720	535
.308	180	2,620	2,274	1,955	1,666	1,414	2,743	2,066	1,527	1,109	799
.30-06	180	2,700	2,348	2,023	1,727	1466	2,913	2,203	1,635	1,192	859
.300 Savage	180	2,350	2,025	1,728	1,467	1,252	2,207	1,639	1,193	860	626
.300 Win. Mag.	180	2,960	2,745	2,540	2,344	2,157	3,501	3,011	2,578	2,196	1,859
.300 Win. Mag.	200	2,800	2,570	2,350	2,150	1,950	3,480	2,935	2,460	2,050	1,690
.300 Wthby Mag.	180	3,120	2,866	2,627	2,400	2,184	3,890	3,284	2,758	2,301	1,905
.300 Wthby Mag.	200	2,925	2,690	2,467	2,254	2,052	3,799	3,213	2,701	2,256	1,870
28mm Rem. Mag.	200	2,900	2,623	2,361	2,115	1,885	3,734	3,054	2,476	1,987	1,577
.338 Win. Mag.	225	2,800	2,560	2,330	2,110	1,900	3,915	3,265	2,700	2,220	1,800
.338 Win. Mag.	250	2,660	2,400	2,150	1,910	1,690	3,925	3,185	2,555	2,055	1,590
.348 Win.	200	2,520	2,215	1,931	1,672	1,443	2,820	2,178	1,656	1,241	925
.358 Win.	200	2,490	2,171	1,876	1,610	1,379	2,753	2,093	1,563	1,151	844
.35 Whelen	250	2,400	2,197	2,005	1,823	1,652	3,197	2,680	2,230	1,844	1,515
.375 H&H Mag.	270	2,690	2,420	2,166	1,928	1,707	4,337	3,510	2,812	2,228	1,747

BOWS & ARROWS

lack bear hunting with bow and arrow has grown in popularity in recent years. One reason is the fact that a large percentage of nonresident bowhunters choose to pursue bruins on guided bait hunts, where shot opportunities and success rates are much better than either spot-and-stalk or do-it-yourself hunts. Using archery gear is also popular with many bowhunters who pursue bears with dogs on guided hunting trips. And there are many of us who enjoy the tough

Treestands are commonly employed by bait hunters, who like to get high above a bear's line of sight and smell while waiting for a big bruin to come in. Make sure your stand is set in the shade and has plenty of natural camouflage around it.

challenge of trying to spot a bear, then stalk in close enough for a good bow shot.

As a member of the North American Hunting Club's Bowhunting Advisory Council, I receive a fair number of letters from readers asking about the appropriate tackle to use when hunting a variety of big game species. A common question involves black bear hunting. I've seen several dozen black bears taken with archery gear over the past two decades, experience that has helped me formulate some definite opinions on the right stuff for a black bear hunt.

MATCH THE HATCH

As is the case with firearms hunting, there are essentially two types of black bear bowhunts. The most common are bait and hound hunts, in which shots generally come at very close range—usually 20 yards or less. The other is the spot-and-stalk hunt, where shot opportunities can stretch the limits of your shooting skills.

You don't necessarily need the same setup for each situation. Unless you shoot a real "soft" setup, your standard treestand deer hunting setup is adequate for bait and hound hunts. On spot-and-stalk hunts, a bit flatter-shooting bow-and-arrow setup is a better choice.

Also keep in mind the size of the bears you expect to encounter. The large-bodied bears living in Alaska, western Canada and down the West Coast, as well as the bruins found in the Carolinas, parts of Arizona, and in other areas known for monster bears, are tougher animals to shoot through than the small-bodied bears encountered most frequently in central Canada and similar environs.

In all cases, it is important to remember that bears have almost indestructible leg bones, virtually impenetrable scapulas, and super-sturdy rib bones. Their muscles are thick and dense, their hair long and luxurious. It takes a fair amount of kinetic energy, broadheads with strong ferrules and scalpel-sharp blades, and precise shot placement, to achieve the deep penetration and the terminal performance necessary for a quick, humane death.

BOWS FOR BEARS

In this day and age of high-performance hoopla, all too many archers concern themselves with sizzling arrow speed while forgetting about the importance of deep penetration, reliability and the significance of silence when choosing a

In most instances, the same bow-and-arrow setup you use for white-tailed deer hunting will get the job done on black bears.

Spot-and-stalk hunters might have to shoot out to 40 yards or so. Be sure your bow has a 40-yard pin and that you can consistently make that kind of shot.

new compound bow. For black bear hunting, get a bow that's forgiving, easy to draw and hold, and that consistently places the shaft on target at moderate ranges. Avoid the whiz-bang speed bow that's noisy and groups arrows erratically.

Generally speaking, you need a bow you can draw smoothly and hold for an extended period of time. If you are a spot-and-stalk bowhunter, you'll be best served if you can draw and shoot from your knees or with your body twisted at an odd angle. And remember that while most bears are taken at close range, spot-and-stalk hunting shots can be on the long side too. The first bear I shot on an archery stalk hunt was taken at 37 yards, the last at 10 yards. It will pay to meticulously tune your bow-and-arrow setup, then extend your own personal maximum shooting range.

Both one- and two-cam bows are excellent choices for all bowhunting, including bear hunts. The increased efficiency of modern compound bows has eliminated the need for pulling Herculean draw weights to achieve high arrow speed. For black bear hunting, I prefer a minimum draw weight of about 55 pounds, though my own bear bows are set at

I prefer carbon arrows for bear hunting with the belief that they penetrate better than fatter aluminum shafts. Both the Easton A/C/C (top) and Beman ICS (bottom) are excellent choices.

70 pounds. Companies like Browning, Bear/Jennings, Custom Shooting Systems, Darton, High Country Archery, Hoyt, McPherson Archery, Mathews Archery, Martin, Oneida and PSE, among others, all build quality bows suitable for black bear hunts.

What about traditional bows? I say: Why not? Many good black bears are taken each year with both recurves and longbows. These bows are great when treestand hunting over baits, and skilled stalkers can get close enough to use them as well. If you're a traditional archer, don't shy away from bear hunting because you think you're "underbowed."

ARROW SHAFTS & BROADHEADS

Both aluminum and carbon shafts are excellent hunting arrows. I personally prefer carbon shafts for all my bowhunting, believing they are tougher and penetrate better than comparable aluminum shafts. That said, I've taken several black bears with aluminum arrow shafts too. The bottom line: Match the shaft to the bow and use a setup you have confidence in.

As mentioned earlier, black bears have thick muscles, long hair and big bones. Only top-quality broadheads with stout ferrules and blades so sharp they scare you are acceptable. My favorite replaceable-blade heads come from companies like Barrie Archery, New Archery Products, Satellite, Golden Key-Futura, Muzzy, Game Tracker, AHT and Archer's Ammo. I prefer fixed-blade heads from companies like Elk Mountain Archery, Zwickey, Delta and Magnus. The key is a super-strong ferrule, like Barrie's titanium version, or high-quality aluminum and strong, sharp blades.

Recurves and longbows will kill black bears handily. Taking (and making) the right shot is key.

Black bears have thick hair, huge muscles, and leg bones like steel pipes. Use only broadheads with super-strong ferrules, and blades so sharp they scare you. Replaceable-blade broadheads like these are the most popular choice.

Given sharp blades, most any strong broadhead will do the job on bears. The bottom line then becomes finding a broadhead that shoots well with your bow.

Controversy continues to rage regarding the use of mechanical broadheads on black bear hunts. After tracking and losing a disproportionate number of bears hit with mechanicals, I know some

The very best mechanical broadheads will take even the largest black bears cleanly. The most important factor is arrow placement.

experienced guides who will not allow them in their hunting camps. However, I have friends who swear by them. In some states they are illegal, so be sure to check the regulations before using them. If this head design floats your boat, be sure to use only the best. Mechanical broadheads from companies like Barrie Archery, Mar-Den, Sonoran Bowhunting Products, Game Tracker and New Archery Products, among others, fit that description.

BOW SIGHTS

Black bears are dark animals usually taken on the cusp of daylight, often in shaded areas or thick brush. For that reason, you need sight pins you can easily see in the worst light conditions imaginable—and that means fiber-optic sight pins. Also, make sure your bow sight can be secured tightly to the bow's riser, has a rugged pin guard, and has a minimum of moving parts that can rattle loose.

I've shot sights from Sonoran Bowhunting

Because a large proportion of shots at black bears occur on the cusp of daylight, using a bow sight with fiber-optic pins makes sense. A pendulum sight (top, left) is a great choice for treestand hunting.

Products for the past several years with excellent results. Sights from companies like TruGlo, Sight Master, Fine-Line, Browning, PSE, Jennings Archery, Cobra, Toxonics and Montana Black Gold are other examples of top-quality bow sights.

For treestand hunters, a pendulum bow sight will work extremely well—those from Keller and Savage Systems are excellent. Peep sights must let in maximum available light too. The Cee-Peep, Fine-Line Sta-Brite, Game Tracker Dusk Vision, Shepley Peep and Shurz-A-Peep are great.

ARCHERY ACCESSORIES

In my mind, a bow-attached quiver is the way to go for all bowhunting, though many treestand hunters like a detachable quiver. To each his own. Most bow companies offer quivers matched to their specific bow models.

Arrow rests can be a major source of bowhunting frustration. Choose rests with the fewest moving parts, least number of screws and easiest

adjustments. Golden Key-Futura, New Archery Products, Savage Systems, Mathews Archery and Bodoodle make excellent hunting rests.

A bow sling makes packing your bow to and from a treestand, or lugging it when you're out on a spot-and-stalk hunt, easy as pie.

There are a myriad of different release aids available. The most popular design is the caliper wrist strap-type release aid, my choice for more than a decade, primarily because the strap keeps the release from falling off when I'm moving quickly to get into position for a shot when stalking. There are many excellent releases out there, including those from Pro Release, Scott Archery, Golden Key-Futura, Jim Fletcher Archery, Tru-Fire, Winn Archery, Jerry Carter and T.R.U. Ball. Regardless of whether you shoot with a release or with fingers, always carry a spare release or finger tab in your day pack or pants pocket, just in case.

It's also essential to carry something that makes it easy for you to check the wind constantly: Try Knight & Hale Windfloaters, a butane lighter, or a small puff bottle filled with unscented talc or cornstarch. Unless you can beat the wind, and with it a bear's superb nose, you'll never have the chance to launch a single arrow.

Some treestand hunters use a string tracker to help them recover their bears more easily. String

The black bear's number-one defense is its sense of smell. Constantly monitoring the wind is critical to your success. API's Windfloaters are a great tool for this job.

trackers work well, the caveat being that they limit the range at which you can shoot (about 30 yards being maximum), and you have to make sure to sight in your bow with the tracking device because it will cause arrows to fly differently than without one. Game Tracker makes the best known of these devices.

Get the Range Right

*I*n all bowhunting, knowing the exact distance to the target is the key to making a good, killing shot. That's why carrying a laser rangefinder is so important.

There are two kinds of rangefinders—coincidence and laser. Coincidence units, popularized by Ranging, Inc., work on the principle of triangulation. They have two windows and a system of prisms and lenses that produce two images you see when you look through the viewfinder. You simply turn a pre-calibrated dial, stopping when the two images coincide and become one, then read the distance off the dial. With a bit of practice, these types of units can be quite accurate.

But today the laser rangefinder is a far superior tool. Laser units send out a beam of light—a laser beam—that is reflected off the target object. The amount of time it takes for the beam to go out and return to the rangefinder unit is mathematically translated into the precise distance from the unit to the target.

Coincidence rangefinders are less expensive than laser units but are tougher to use and are not quite as accurate. But in skilled hands, they work well.

Today's laser rangefinders are precise to within plus or minus 1 or 2 yards at their advertised distances. They're compact, and can be worn either around the neck with a strap, or carried in a soft belt pouch. They work on a standard 9-volt battery that will give hundreds of "shots" before wearing down. They can also take a fair amount of field abuse and keep on ticking.

The best units I've used to date are from Bushnell, including the Yardage Pro 400, Yardage Pro 800 and my favorite, the Yardage Pro Compact 600. The Leica 800 and Nikon Buckmasters 800 are other excellent units. The $200 or $300 you'll spend on a quality rangefinder will be a good investment: Not only will it help you get a bear, but it will also be useful in many other kinds of hunting.

A laser rangefinder should be standard equipment for any bear bowhunter. Precise shot placement is critical when bear hunting, and a laser rangefinder will help you achieve just that.

BLACKPOWDER BEARS

Hunting bears with a muzzleloader is like stepping back in time. On the frontier in the 1800s, black bears were a staple of both Native Americans and settlers, who hunted them with both flintlock and, later, percussion muzzleloading rifles. Today, thanks to the introduction of the in-line muzzleloader, blackpowder, one-shot hunting has measurably increased in popularity.

I took my first muzzleloader black bear about 20 years ago when I was carrying a bear tag in my pocket on an elk hunt "just in case." My rifle was a .54 caliber percussion Hawken replica I built myself from a kit, loaded with that fancy new (at the time) Pyrodex blackpowder substitute and a conical slug made by a then-new but now well-known company named Buffalo Bullets.

It's a sign of the times, I guess, that today I bear hunt with an in-line muzzleloader. If you have never tried muzzleloader hunting, or have hunted deer or elk with a front-stuffer but are concerned that your rifle may not be up to snuff for bear hunting, here is some advice on choosing the right rifle/load combination.

Modern in-line muzzleloaders are superb tools, capable of consistently taking black bears at ranges of up to 150 yards. Stainless steel metalwork is a good choice for the wet conditions often encountered.

RIFLES

By far, muzzleloading rifles featuring an in-line ignition system are the most common used by modern hunters. But another style is also popular: the sidelock. Sidelock percussion rifles are the kind you see in the movies or read about in books of the Old West. They are of the classic Hawken design, and remain popular today with traditionalists who want to step back in time and hunt the way the old-time trappers and explorers did. Thompson/Center, CVA and Dixie Gun Works, among others, all make excellent rifles of this type.

The in-line muzzleloader is the

Tony Knight started the in-line muzzleloader revolution with his MK-85, and he shows us here just how effective these tools can be when hunting even the largest black bears.

rifle of choice for serious, modern bear hunters who don't care about tradition as much as they do reliable performance and superb ballistics. Tony Knight, a gunsmith from Lancaster, Missouri, is such a man. He built the first modern in-line muzzleloading rifle in 1983. In 1985, he introduced the Knight MK-85, which set the tone for both the industry and the hunters it served.

The MK-85 had modern rifle features, including receivers drilled and tapped for scope mounts, and an adjustable trigger. Plus, a removable breech plug greatly simplified cleaning and permitted hunters to push an unfired charge out the breech at day's end, instead of having to either pull the ball or bullet out the barrel or fire the rifle, which meant a half-hour's cleaning session.

Other makers like White, Thompson/Center and CVA soon joined in. Today there is a raft of additional companies like Traditions, Gonic Arms, Markesbery Muzzleloaders, Navy Arms, Dixie Gun Works, Austen & Halleck, Remington, Ruger, Mossberg and Marlin that all sell quality in-line muzzleloaders.

In-lines are the best choice for serious, no-nonsense big game hunting, including black bear hunting. For bears, choose a rifle of at least .50 caliber. A .54 caliber packs even more punch. Regardless of which you choose, it's most important to work up an accurate load, learn to shoot the rifle well and get as close as possible before squeezing the trigger.

PROJECTILES & PROPELLANTS

A patched round ball—the kind used by riflemen from the earliest days until the early 1800s—is still shot by some big game hunters. However, savvy muzzleloaders use either conical bullets or, where legal, sabot-encased conical bullets. These bullets provide maximum penetration and kinetic energy transfer for clean kills on the largest bruins.

Many different companies offer quality muzzleloading bullets today, including well-known blackpowder rifle makers like Thompson/Center, CVA, Traditions, Knight Rifles and Remington, as well as specialists like Buffalo Bullet Co., Muzzleload Magnum Products (MMP), Precision Rifle Bullets, Northern Precision, Parker Productions, Black Belt Bullets from Big Bore Express, Game Buster Bullets, and well-known and easily recognizable centerfire ammunition and bullet makers like Hornady, Barnes, Nosler, Swift Bullet Co. and Lyman.

The propellant choices are two: traditional blackpowder or Pyrodex, a synthetic propellant

Conical bullets—both those encased in a sabot and those without—are far and away the best choice for black bear hunting, providing the maximum kinetic energy and penetration, which is exactly what you need when hunting these tough animals. Some traditionalists still go the round-ball route.

Synthetic Pyrodex and traditional blackpowder both work well as muzzleloading rifle propellants.

major gun makers, but also by well-known after-market accessory manufacturers like Uncle Mike's and Bridger's Best.

One excellent accessory item is the Dry Fire Breech Protector, a simply designed product that keeps moisture out of the breech area of many models of in-line muzzleloaders. Another is the Traditions EZ Unloader, which uses a blast of compressed air at the breech end to push powder and projectile down and out the barrel when unloading at day's end.

Taking it one step further, many experienced shooters are looking to upgrade their sighting systems. TruGlo's excellent fiber-optic Illuminator, Magnum Muzzle Dot and Muzzle Dot sights are superb choices for hunting with open sights. Some rifle makers offer them as standard fare, and you can also get them as an aftermarket replacement part. Williams Gun Sight Company's Firesight is another fiber-optic sight that's made of steel, not plastic.

Some hunters replace their factory open sights with a peep sight like Thompson/Center's Tang Peep Sight. And while some optics manufacturers like Burris, Bushnell, Leupold and Simmons produce scopes touted specifically for modern muzzleloaders, many in-line shooters top their rifles

that performs like blackpowder but is less pervious to the evil effects of moisture. Goex and Elephant Black Powder are the two most popular brands of traditional blackpowder. But today most muzzleloaders choose Hodgdon's Pyrodex, which is available in both traditional granulated form and Pyrodex Pellets, a pre-measured charge that comes compressed in easy-to-use pellet form that you simply drop down the barrel. Pyrodex is not legal in all states, so be sure to check the regulations, but where I can use them, convenient Pyrodex Pellets are my first choice, hands down.

MUZZLELOADING ACCESSORIES

Muzzleloader hunters require their own specialized accessories for cleaning and loading their rifles and for packing their "stuff."

Most blackpowder rifle makers offer cleaning supplies—like ramrods and attachments, patches and cleaning solvents—and often package them in kit form. These and other items, like powder measures, powder flasks, speed loaders, percussion caps, cappers, possibles bags and pouches and other accessories, are offered not only by many

Blackpowder hunters have three rifle types to choose from: flintlocks, percussions and in-lines (top to bottom). For maximum effectiveness, where legal, in-lines are the way to go.

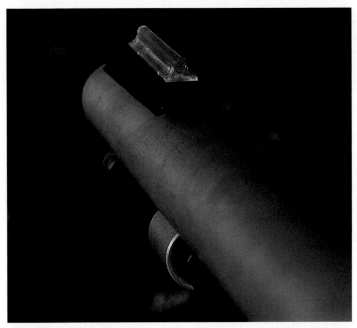

with the same top-quality variable rifle scope they use on their centerfire rifles. Scopes are not legal in all states, so be sure to check regulations before adding one.

HEADING AFIELD

When heading afield, keep it simple. I carry five pre-loaded speed loaders filled with premeasured Pyrodex charges or Pyrodex Pellets and bullets, a short starter and a full capper. I also pack a combination nipple/breech plug wrench, several clean, pre-lubed patches and a small amount of bore cleaner (should I have to clean the rifle in the field), and a couple small balloons that can be fitted over the barrel if it starts raining. That's it. Everything else, including a spare ramrod and full cleaning kit, is kept at base camp.

Adding a fiber-optic front sight to your muzzleloader will make it easier to line up an accurate shot on the dark body of a big bear as the sun goes down. Standard metal sights just won't get the job done.

Muzzleloading Equipment Check List

☑ Rifle

☑ Percussion caps (or primers)

☑ Capper

☑ Blackpowder or Pyrodex (or pellets)

☑ Powder measure

☑ Powder flask

☑ Bullets

☑ Short bullet starter

☑ Synthetic ramrod

☑ Nipple/breech plug wrench

☑ Pre-lubed patches

☑ Bullet lube

☑ Spare eyeglasses

☑ Speed loaders

☑ Small balloons (for barrel protection)

☑ Cleaning supplies (powder solvent, clean patches, ramrod attachments, light gun oil)

HANDGUN HUNTING

*I*t had been a long, tough climb up the 45-degree slope, fighting through thick coastal Alaska alders and scrambling over slick rock ledges. Two hours into it, I finally broke out above the brush line and quickly began glassing. I had spotted a nice bear from far below and was hoping I could catch him out feeding once I had made the tortuous climb.

I did not see the bear right off, but that didn't worry me much. It was mid-morning, a time when feeding bears like to find a nice flat ledge to lie on and rest. I took off my pack, settled in and started searching. It was a full hour before I saw the bear again, munching on fresh, green spring grass and digging up the roots of skunk cabbage. He was a nice one, and I wanted him.

Moving into position 100 yards from him, I used my backpack to craft a solid rest, then laid my Thompson Contender single-shot pistol, chambered in .35 Rem., over the top and got into

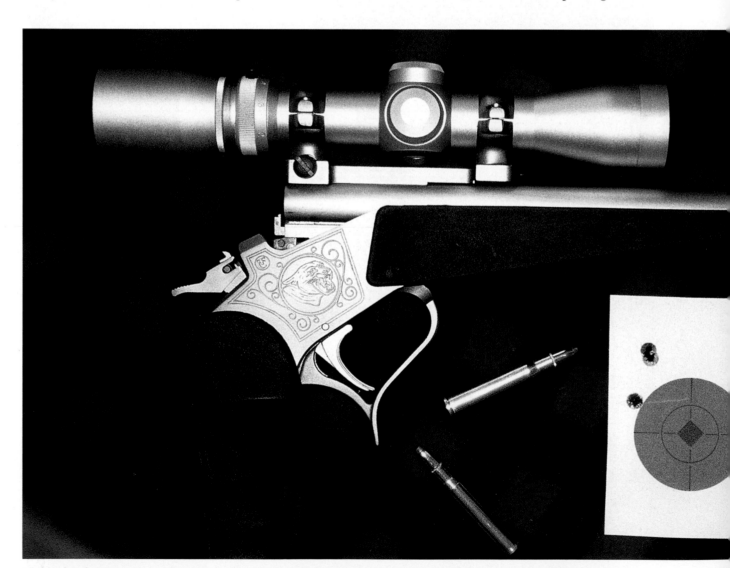

Modern handguns are outstanding bear medicine. When shots might be on the long side, using a scoped single-shot specialty pistol like the Thompson/Center Contender will allow you to take bears out past the 100-yard mark.

the prone position. With the scope turned up to 7X, I found the bear in the lens, settled the crosshairs just behind his front shoulder, waited for him to turn broadside and squeezed the trigger. The 200-grain Core-Lokt bullet really thumped him. Now it was time to skin and bone the bear and pack him back down the mountain.

There are a select number of black bear hunters who like to pursue big bruins with handguns. Given the limited range of revolvers, it's a real challenge. Hunters using single-shot specialty handguns and some revolvers with a lot of downrange "pop," such as the .454 Casull, have a better chance on spot-and-stalk hunts. In fact, most handgunners hunt bears either over baits or behind hounds where, like bowhunters, they know that when their opportunity comes it will be at close range at a calm bear that will give

them a broadside shot.

Handgun hunters generally choose between two pistol types—revolvers and single-shot specialty pistols. Here's a look at each.

REVOLVERS

Most revolver hunters hunt over baits or behind hounds, and like to bring their "home defense" pistols with them. That's fine, except that I don't believe a .357 Mag. is enough gun for bears. My own personal minimum is the .41, though the .44 Mag. is even better. The powerful .454 Casull is superb, but few people own one and fewer can handle the massive recoil this cartridge generates. I do have friends who can and are excellent shots at 100 to 125 yards with their scoped Casulls, but hunters who use a .41 or .44 Mag. try to keep their shots inside 75 yards. Ideally, they'll get closer.

Revolver hunters have been blessed in recent years by the development of ammunition and bullets specifically designed for big game hunting. These jacketed bullets will penetrate deeply, yet expand rapidly once inside the chest cavity, at revolver velocities. Winchester, Federal and Remington make excellent factory ammunition that's designed expressly for this purpose and will cleanly take black bears.

SINGLE-SHOT SPECIALTY PISTOLS

The single-shot specialty pistol, which is really nothing more than a compact rifle with a shorter barrel and without the lengthy butt stock, was developed by three notable gun authorities: my friend and one of the country's finest gun writers, the late Bob Milek; former Remington public rela-

Jeff Sullivan took this beautiful cinnamon bear with his .44 Magnum revolver. Revolvers like the .41 and .44 Mag. are excellent for bears under 50 yards.

I took this dandy bruin with my Thompson/Center Contender in .35 Remington, a handgun/cartridge combination that has accounted for several dandy bears over the years.

tions guru Dick Dietz; and legendary stock-maker Steve Herrett.

Single-shot handguns have grown rapidly in popularity since their introduction in the early 1980s. The best specialty pistols feature crisp triggers, well-built stocks and accurate barrels between 10 and 16 inches long. There are two types of actions: break-open, popularized by the Thompson/Center Contender and Encore; and bolt-action, developed by Milek, Dietz and Herrett, and popularized by the Remington XP-100. Today there are other handguns of this type, notably the Savage Striker. Some, like the modern XP-100, have blind magazines. Many have synthetic stocks.

Though considered a handgun, in truth these firearms must be fired from a solid rest to achieve accurate bullet flight. And accurate they are. I've seen several that can place five shots inside a half-dollar at 100 yards all day long. They are also chambered for some of the finest big game hunting cartridges ever developed, including the 7mm-08, .308 and .30-06, as well as a host of wildcat cartridges designed to give near-rifle performance. The most popular line of wildcat cartridges was designed by well-known handgun hunter J.D. Jones. In all cases, they can be loaded with spitzer-type hunting bullets designed to perform exactly like those found in centerfire rifle ammunition on

deer-sized game. In many cases, the exact same ammunition can be used.

Single-shot specialty pistols are fun to shoot and, in the hands of a skilled marksman, are as effective on black bears as any firearm ever developed. Each spring, I take my Contender bear hunting, a pastime that brings me great pleasure and keeps my freezer filled.

SCOPES & ACCESSORIES

Most handgun hunters add a scope to their weapon. Many good scopes and mounts, designed especially for handguns, are available. Make sure you go with one of these specially-designed products (not an old rifle scope) to get the proper eye relief, accuracy and performance out of your setup. You're in for a big disappointment if you try to use an old rifle scope on a new pistol.

Some accessories that many handgunners deem necessary include shoulder holsters, and aiming aids to lend a steady rest. Michael's of Oregon offers one of the most comfortable and accessible shoulder holsters I've ever seen. You can get a lightweight Harris bipod and attach it to the forend of some single-shot pistols, for a rock-solid field rest. Shooting sticks (I like the ones from Stoney Point Products) also help you gain a steady rest in the field.

Reloading fanatics are in luck too, because reloading dies, brass, bullets and other components are widely available for both standard and wildcat handgun cartridges, allowing you to customize a load that will take care of any bruin on the block.

I love handgun hunting. And when black bears are the quarry, the equation gets that much more exciting. It's a great way to add challenge and enjoyment to your hunt.

When hunting open country with a handgun, the venerable .454 Casull can't be beat. A scope makes it a 100-yard tool.

Select Black Bear Cartridges
Handguns

Cartridge Name	Bullet Weight (grains)	Velocity (fps)				Kinetic Energy (foot-pounds)			
		Muzzle	50 yards	100 yards	200 yards	Muzzle	50 yards	100 yards	200 yards
Revolver Cartridges									
.41 Mag.	175	1,250	1,120	1,029	—	607	488	412	—
.44 Mag.	210	1,250	1,106	1,010	—	729	570	475	—
.44 Mag.	240	1,180	1,081	1,010	—	741	623	543	—
.454 Casull	260	1,800	1,605	1,427	—	1,871	1,485	1,176	—
.454 Casull	300	1,625	1,451	1,308	—	1,759	1,413	1,141	—
Single-Shot Specialty Pistol Cartridges									
.270 Win.	130	3,000	—	2,800	—	2,700	—	2,300	—
7mm-08	140	2,750	—	2,540	—	2,430	—	2,025	—
7-30 Waters	120	2,700	—	2,300	—	1,940	—	1,405	—
.30-30	170	2,200	—	1,850	—	1,830	—	1,320	—
.308	150	2,800	—	2,600	—	2,650	—	2,225	—
.30-06	150	2,875	—	2,650	—	2,800	—	2,400	—
.35 Rem.	200	2,060	—	1,658	—	1,911	—	1,250	—
.45-70 Gov't	300	1,800	—	1,450	—	2,180	—	1,455	—

OPTICS FOR BLACK BEAR HUNTING

lack bears are dark-colored animals that live primarily in thick cover and like to move on the edges of daylight. Imagine trying to glass up a dark blob in the shadows after the sun has dipped below the horizon. Seeing bears under these conditions can be quite difficult. It can also hinder precise placement of your riflescope's crosshairs. Add to that the fact that if a bear rug is your dream, you must carefully look the hide over for rub marks. To top it all off, in many areas you can count on wet weather in the form of rain, fog and/or salt spray that can and will fog up cheap binoculars and scopes so fast it will make your head spin.

By now, you have probably figured out that you need the best optics you can afford when hunting black bears. Here's what to look for.

BINOCULARS & SPOTTING SCOPES

Binoculars should be chosen in terms of the type of hunt you'll be doing. You do not need the same glass for sitting in a treestand over a bait barrel as you need for a spot-and-stalk hunt.

Spot-and-stalk bear hunters need top-quality fogproof, waterproof binoculars and spotting scopes. Using glass with a large objective lens will help find bears when the light gets dim in the evenings, when the bruins are most active.

them all day long without a tripod because they're not over-powered.

On some Western hunts, where glassing game at a mile or more is common, I have used my tripod-mounted 15X60 Zeiss binoculars to spot bears. When sitting over bait or creeping along through thick cover, 7X35 binoculars are excellent, offering a wide field of view and plenty of power to carefully look over a hide for rubs.

Spotting scopes are important on spot-and-stalk hunts. The last thing you want to do is spot a bear with your binoculars, climb a mountain and then, when you get close, find that he is rubbed up. Spotters in the 15-45X and 20-60X class are ideal for this.

RIFLESCOPES

Scopes designed for deer hunting will work well for black bears. Variable scopes in the 2-7X, 2.5-8X, 3-9X and 3.5-10X class are excellent, with those featuring an objective lens of between 40mm and 50mm better than those with smaller objective lenses. If you prefer a fixed-power, a 4X scope will work fine.

I like plex-type reticles for all my hunting and find them especially good for black bears. The thick posts that taper down to thin crosshairs make precise bullet placement easy, even in the dawn, dusk and shadows. A post-and-crosshair design is also good. Where legal, using a lighted dot is excellent, especially on bait hunts, where the distance is short and bears are notorious for coming in at slap dark.

When using a spotting scope, be sure to have along a sturdy tripod that has extendable legs sturdy enough to hold the scope steady when the wind blows. Spotters make evaluating trophy quality from a distance easy.

Spot-and-stalk hunters should continually glass edge cover for emerging bears.

Regardless, one key is to choose binoculars that gather the maximum amount of available light. This means a glass with a large twilight factor (see sidebar on page 46).

For spot-and-stalk hunting, 8X to 10X binoculars are an excellent choice. They offer enough power to let you find distant bears, yet you can use

BUY QUALITY

When it comes to the quality of hunting optics, you definitely get what you pay for. More expensive optics have better glass and higher-quality coatings on that glass; both features will pay off when conditions are poor. Better optics will also be less likely to fog up or leak in bad weather. Today there are a slug of top-notch binoculars, spotting scopes and riflescopes to choose from. Companies like Bausch & Lomb, Nikon, Steiner, Fujinon, Leupold, Simmons, Swarovski, Zeiss, Kahles, Swift, Leica and Leitz, among others, make excellent products.

Calculating Twilight Factor

*T*he twilight factor is the amount of usable light binoculars or spotting scopes transfer to your eyes. The higher the twilight factor, the easier it will be for you to see in low-light conditions.

To calculate the twilight factor, simply divide the diameter of the front, or ocular, lens on the binoculars by the diameter of the smaller, rear lens. Thus, 10X40 binoculars have a twilight factor of 4 (40 divided by 10), 7X35 binoculars have a twilight factor of 5 (35 divided by 7) and compact 10X28 binoculars have a twilight factor of only 2.8 (28 divided by 10). The 7X35s, with a twilight factor of 5, will offer your eyes the most light in low-light situations.

Because of the physical limitations of the human eye, you can go overboard here. Experts believe the maximum amount of light the human eye can use is equivalent to a twilight factor between about 5 and 6. Thus, while 8X56 binoculars might have a twilight factor of 7, some of the light transmitted cannot be used by the eye. Because this is an individual thing, you should compare different binoculars at your local sporting goods store before buying. Take them outside at dusk and glass distant objects. You'll see the difference.

Twilight factor is also important when choosing a riflescope. Generally speaking, scopes with the largest objective lens will gather the most light. Also remember that when turning up the power of a variable scope, the amount of light transmitted to the eye decreases. For black bear hunting, I prefer scopes with at least a 40mm objective lens.

Using binoculars with a high twilight factor makes it easier to spot bears at dawn and dusk, when the animals are most active. To calculate the twilight factor, divide the diameter of the front lens by the diameter of the smaller rear lens.

SHOT PLACEMENT

egardless of your choice of weapon or the game you are hunting, there is nothing more important at the moment of truth than precise shot placement. It takes practice and discipline to make the shot count in all hunting situations. I have seen experienced hunters and excellent shooters make more poor shots at bears than at any other game animal. Perhaps it is a subliminal fear of bears. Who knows? I just know that shooting at a bear is no time for anything but your best effort. That means following a shooting system that will allow you to precisely place your bullet or broadhead in the bear's boiler room.

B.R.A.S.S.

I always run down a mental checklist before squeezing the trigger of a firearm or releasing the string of my bow. This helps me control my excitement and adrenaline rush so that I stay calm enough to set my sights exactly where they should be. In the military they teach you to shoot by the acronym BRASS: Breathe, Relax, Aim, Sight picture, Squeeze the trigger. It works like this:

Breathe. Take a deep breath to relax and to keep your body from bouncing, thus moving the sight picture like a rubber duck on a rough pond. Before squeezing the trigger, let out about a third of that breath.

Relax. Athletes know that they perform at their best when their muscles are relaxed, not tense. Keep your shooting muscles firm, but relaxed. You've made the shot a thousand times in practice, so why worry you can't make it now?

Regardless of your choice of weapon, shot placement is everything when you're bear hunting. Place your projectile through both lungs, and the bear will pile up in less than 45 seconds.

Aim. No matter what kind of sights you're using, there is a right and wrong place to aim when it comes to aligning the sights on the target. Don't panic! And don't shoot before aiming.

Sight picture. The accompanying photographs will help you know where to aim. On broadside bears, keep the sights just behind the front leg bone. On quartering-away bears, draw an imaginary line from the onside hide to the off-side shoulder. That will take out both lungs. Keep your shots from the centerline of the chest to the lower third of the chest, no more than 6 to 9 inches behind the front leg.

Squeeze the trigger. Place the trigger of your

The best shot you can get on a black bear is the standing broadside shot, regardless of your hunting weapon. Strive to place your projectile just behind the front leg of this bear, about halfway down his body, and you'll cleanly take out both lungs.

Hunting Black Bears

firearm or archery release aid just outside the last joint of the index finger, not on or behind the joint. Now squeeze it smoothly until the weapon goes off. Make sure you follow through; that is, keep your head down while trying to retain the sight picture despite recoil.

See? There's nothing to it. When bear hunting, you generally have plenty of time to make the shot. Don't hurry. Relax. Remember the BRASS system, and the bear will soon be yours.

A quartering-away angle is an excellent shot for bear hunters—especially bowhunters. Try to center your shot on the off-front leg, halfway down the body, and you'll get both lungs.

Quartering-to angles are poor shots on bears, unless you are using a powerful rifle or handgun cartridge. On this bear, place the bullet just inside the front leg halfway down the body for a heart/lung shot. Bowhunters and muzzleloaders have no shot here!

Chapter 3

BEAR BAITING

*I*t was getting darker by the minute when I heard the cracking of a twig break the stillness of twilight time.

I moved only my eyes, shifted my gaze left and quickly picked up the bear. He was a dandy—a block-headed, roly-poly boar heading for my ground set. "It's him, finally," I thought, thinking back to countless hours spent scouting for this site, prepping it, setting a stand and hauling hundreds of pounds of bait by backpack over six weeks. I'd played chess with this big boar for three weeks, but all I'd seen were the big tracks and scat piles he left. Until tonight, after I'd changed things around a bit and given him something new.

When he got to the bait he paused, put his nose high into the air and sniffed for danger. Satisfied, he got to digging. When he turned and gave me a quartering-away angle I released my arrow. Checkmate. The perfect ending to an exciting and difficult season of bear baiting.

Bear baiting is under attack by anti-hunters and some people who consider themselves serious hunters too. Its opponents accuse bear baiting of being too easy and unethical. Yet I find it one of the most challenging and enjoyable forms of big game hunting I do every year. It's a chess game, a contest that will teach you as much about black bears and their habits as any other type of bear hunting you can do.

If you've never hunted bears over bait, it is hard to understand the allure of the game. And baiting on your own is much different than taking a guided bait hunt. The amount of work necessary to do it right is staggering. Having the discipline to pass small boars and sows is extremely satisfying. And when it all comes together, and a big, mature boar with a flawless hide shows himself, the proud feeling of accomplishment is on par with all other forms of bear hunting.

Bear baiting. It's controversial and it is anything but easy. Want to learn how to do it right? Then read on …

WHY BAIT BEARS?

It takes lots of hard work to bait mature boars successfully. Bear baiting is the best way I know of to selectively harvest only mature boars, a big reason many game managers support the practice.

*I*t was a cat-and-mouse game we were playing, the big boar and I. I knew he was there, and he knew I was there too. My trail timer had shown that he came to the bait several times a day, which meant he was living close by. But even when one of my buddies sat on the stand for hours on end, the bear wouldn't show. Next day, the timer would confirm that the bear came in 30 minutes after the hunter walked out.

It was time to take matters to the next level. Mike and I waited for a few days, letting the weather stabilize until we had a calm, clear evening. During that time I went in and re-baited every evening, then left. On this day we went to the stand about 7:30 p.m., and as Mike climbed into the tree-stand and got settled in, I re-baited, taking my time and fussing about until he was organized and quiet. Then I walked out, climbed into the truck and drove off.

"Sure enough, about 45 minutes after you left I heard a branch crack, and pretty soon I could see the bear coming through the brush," Mike said. "He was cautious as an old buck deer, sniffing the air and listening hard. Once he decided it was okay, he walked straight to the barrel, and when he started brushing the limbs off the opening, I drew the bow. The angle was perfect, and I let it fly. He woofed, spun around and ran into the bush. I heard him fall not 50 yards away. It took me a while to calm down before I could safely climb out of the stand and go find him, I was so excited."

He should have been excited. The old boar was Mike's first-ever bow kill. The bear had a perfect, jet-black hide with no rubs that squared 6 feet; the animal weighed about 250 pounds. For the area of coastal Alaska we were hunting, he was a real dandy.

I have baited spring black bears hard every year since the late 1980s. It is one of the most enjoyable forms of hunting I do. Yet despite the common perception that it is a slam-dunk way to kill big bears, I have found that fooling mature boars is anything but easy.

Baiting is time-consuming hard work, and success is anything but guaranteed. Baiting does, however, offer many advantages that other forms of black bear hunting do not. If you are a novice bear hunter living in a state that allows bear baiting, or if you are planning a spring hunt to one of those states that does allow baiting, you should consider giving it a try. Here are some of the reasons why.

SELECTIVE HARVEST

I've taken a lot of black bears over the years, both for their hides and for their delicious meat. I live in some of the best black bear country in the world, and that makes it easier for me than for most folks to hunt black bears often. For that reason, I make it a point to shoot nothing but mature boars. For me, hunting black bears over bait is trophy hunting at its finest. For every bear I've personally taken over bait, I've let at least another dozen walk. Those were bears that either were small, had imperfect hides, or were sows or sows with cubs.

That's one of the big advantages of bait hunting. If you are a patient, persistent hunter, you can closely look the bears over and let the small boars and sows go if they do not meet your personal standards. Game managers love this. As they

Hunting over bait is great because there's plenty of time to decide whether the bear is a boar—and big enough for your desires—before you draw the string or raise your rifle.

do with all big game species in North America, these biologists hope sport hunters harvest more males than females. But because bears, unlike ungulates, have no antlers that make it easy to distinguish males from females, game managers do restrict or eliminate the harvest of females. But bait hunters who do their homework and take their time on stand can easily tell the difference, and let the females walk.

Unfortunately, this is not happening across the board. Statistics from states like Idaho, Colorado and Alaska show that baiters take as many females as hunters using other methods. Speculation for this runs rampant, but two reasons come to mind.

First, many bait hunters are novice bear hunters who have never seen many, if any, bears. To them, all black bears look big. Second, many of these same hunters are on guided bait hunts. They've paid their money, and after sitting on a stand all week long without seeing a bear, if a sow happens to appear late in the week, they are going to get their money's worth. Rather than come back again and harvest a big boar—most bear hunters only hunt black bears one time—they settle for a small female and are happy to have it.

The choice is theirs, but in my mind that's a shame. If you hunt over bait, it is in the sport's best interest that you make a conscious effort to select males for harvest.

HIGH-QUALITY SHOTS

If you've ever tried spot-and-stalk hunting for black bears in the intermountain West or in the rugged coastal mountains of British Columbia and Alaska, you know how tough it can be to get into position for a quality shot at an undisturbed bear. Often you will spot the bruin late in the afternoon but at a distance, and closing to within comfortable range either before he moves back into the thick brush or before darkness falls can be problematic.

This is especially true if you are a bowhunter or hunting with a short-range firearm like a revolver. And once you get within a comfortable distance to make the shot, the bear has to present the right shot angle. If bears are up feeding, they are moving constantly, pausing long enough for a shot only occasionally. Then there is the wind, which

It's common to see a bear scratching his back on a sapling, at a bait pile. Once big bears encounter a bait site they like, they often move in and take over the place, turning the bait into their own private dining room.

It takes a lot of bait to draw bears in, and then keep them coming back for more.

in the mountains is about as trustworthy as a politician's promises. So many things can go wrong.

When a bear commits to bait, however, all that changes. Now the bear is concentrating on the bait, and not worried about you. If the bait is set up right, he will have to paw his way through some brush, logs or other barriers before reaching the food. To do this, he will have to position his body so that he is either broadside or slightly quartering away from you. Because the stand is set no more than 20 to 30 yards from the bait, the shot should be a slam dunk.

It is the chance for these high-quality shots that makes bear baiting so advantageous, especially for archers and revolver hunters. You're elevated above the bear and he can't see you, so you can move your body enough to get comfortable and make the kind of shot you've made a thousand times in practice. After the hit, you can calmly and silently watch the bear as he runs off, and often you can hear him go down. It doesn't get any better.

BEAR SCHOOL

One thing I really like about bear baiting is the opportunity to observe a lot of different bears for extended periods of time. After watching a black bear lift a log off my bait set (which had taken the strength of two grown men to place in position) as if it were a feather, I developed an appreciation for the sheer power of a black bear's massive front shoulders and front legs.

I've also marveled at how quietly and quickly bears can move through the woods. Bears are as curious as cats and have memories that would rival an elephant's.

Watching the Show

I really enjoy watching sows and cubs while on a bait station stand. The sow-cub bond is everlasting, yet the sow is a dictator that will not hesitate to aggressively spank her children. The cubs are in love with life and are as playful as newborn kittens, chasing and wrestling with each other and hanging onto their mama until she swats them off.

I have seen some crazy things. One time, a pair of cubs got to chasing each other around a tree as fast as they could go, first one way and then the other, woofing and huffing at each other until both fell over, exhausted. On a steep hillside covered with large alders, I watched a yearling cub crawl out onto an alder branch until it bent over so much he couldn't get off. He was hanging there by his two front paws over a 10-foot drop-off, bawling his little head off until he just had to let go. When he bounced and rolled down the hill, his mama gave him the "I told you so" look and went back to her nap. Cubs are a laugh a minute.

Old boars are something quite different. They are as sneaky as the dickens, rarely approaching the bait without first checking the wind and listening for trouble. Many bear baiters I know swear that these bears know when someone is sitting in a treestand or in a ground blind. I've seen old boars walk to the edge of the brush near my bait and stare up into my tree, looking for me, then simply melt back into the brush. And despite their size and power, they can use their front paws as if they were the hands of a brain surgeon, to get into the bait barrel. After a few bear encounters like these, one gains a much greater respect for the intelligence and craftiness of a mature black bear boar.

More than any other facet of bear baiting, it is this chance to observe bears up close that makes it special for me. Every season I learn more about them. If the truth be known, that's why I really love bear hunting—and bear baiting—so much.

One of the big allures of bear baiting is the chance to observe bears being, well, bears. Learning how they act and watching them play is fun. It's like going to school all over again.

A successful bear baiter will haul literally hundreds, if not thousands, of pounds of bait to his sites during the course of the season. Bear baiting is, in reality, a lot of hard work!

Sweets & Meats

When I first started baiting bears, I was under the impression that it was a simple thing. Throw some meat scraps into a barrel, tie it to a tree and prepare to defend yourself as bears from hither and yon invade the area the very next day.

Was I wrong! One thing I have learned: bears have certain preferences for what they eat. There are baits that will draw bears in more quickly than others, and baits that will hold them when others will not. Often what works like gangbusters in one region doesn't work worth a hoot in another. You have to experiment and see what "your" bears like best.

Attractors

Because bears find bait by using their incredible sense of smell, a good bait will put off a lot of odor to draw them in. I prefer that my attractors are not part of the actual food I put out for the bears, though. When bears arrive to eat, I want to give them fresh food.

There are lots of ways to do this. One is to hang a rag soaked in oil of anise. Anise oil has a sickly-sweet smell that carries quite well and really draws in bears. Many commercial bear attractant scents have an oil of anise base. Vanilla, Liquid Smoke and honey also work well. In coastal areas where baitfish, like herring or anchovies, are prevalent

A variety of manufactured products also do a good job attracting bears. When you light these "smoke sticks," they slowly give off a sweet, bear-attracting scent.

and cheap, I will dump 25 to 50 pounds of bait into a burlap sack and hang it high in a tree.

One trick used for years by bear baiters across the continent is the "honey burn." Here baiters use a small backpacker-type stove and an old I-don't-need-this-any-more pot or skillet filled with honey. When the honey is scorched in the pan, it sends off a sweet odor that bears really like. I've done the same thing with a pound of bacon.

I also like to go to my local fast-food restaurant and get five-gallon jugs of used fryer grease. I'll saturate the ground around the bait with this grease, and once the warm sun hits the grease spot, it begins to smell to high heaven. When the bears arrive and walk around on the greasy ground, they'll then leave their own scent trail that other bears can follow to the bait.

A friend hangs a five-gallon jug full of grease from a rope in a tree near his bait and punches a couple of pinholes in the bottom of the jug. This helps attract the bears and, once they get there, gets them excited as they swat and bite the jug trying to get at the grease. It is something to see.

The key to attracting bears is to produce an odor that tells the bears that here is the mother lode of all snack food stores waiting. You can be sure they'll beat feet to get there.

Meat Baits

Bears of all shapes, sizes and descriptions love meat. Just out of hibernation, they are as hungry as a pack of teenagers. Fatty meat can put weight on a bear in a hurry, and he knows it.

Many different types of meats work very well. In the trapping country of Canada, beaver carcasses are used extensively, and bears love them above all other baits. Fat trimmed from beef and pork, as well as meat that can no longer be sold, is superb and can sometimes be obtained from the local butcher shop or supermarket. Fish carcasses also make good bait.

However, there are several problems in using meat baits. First, they are not legal everywhere, so be sure to check regulations before hauling a hundred pounds of trim to your bait station. Second, bears do not like all meat or fish. For example, in

Sex Scents

Bears breed in late spring and early summer, a season that coincides with baiting seasons. For that reason, using a commercial bear sex scent can be quite effective. It's just like making a scent bomb when hunting whitetails during the rut.

James Valley Scents makes the best-known black bear sex scent. I've tried it and found it does work pretty well at times. The downside is that using these types of scents is not legal everywhere, so be sure to check local regulations first.

Many liquid scents and lures are available for bears in the rut. Create scent bombs just like you would when hunting rutting whitetails.

Busted branches and saplings are the calling cards of lusty bruins in search of sows. Time to get out and use sex scents.

coastal Alaska, where black bears love to eat fish, I thought fish would be the answer. So I brought a pile of gray cod carcasses to my bait one year, fig-

Meats can't be beat as bear bait. But you'll have to keep the supply line going—bears don't want maggoty, rotten meat.

uring the bears would go bonkers over it. In fact, they refused to touch it. I saw bears daintily pick up the cod carcasses, move them 10 yards to the side of the bait, then go back and eat peanut butter.

Salmon heads and tails they loved. Go figure.

Third, meat goes sour and gets full of maggots quickly in warm spring weather. I used to think that was great, that the bears would suck up those protein-rich maggots like M&M's. Uh huh. Once the meat goes maggoty, they won't touch it. That's why when I use meat today, I do not put it in a barrel; instead, I use a ground set that I can change when the maggots get bad.

Fourth, if you bait with meats in grizzly country, you had better be prepared to deal with grizzlies. If and when they come to your bait, they will take it over and run off every black bear for miles. They come most often to meat baits, less often to baits with no meat.

Alaska game department officials, who teach bear baiting classes, encourage hunters to use other baits for this very reason. I've seen grizzly-destroyed bait sites that looked like a D8 Cat had worked the ground over. I've also been stuck in my treestand for hours as grizzlies feasted on my baits (it's illegal to take grizzlies over bait in Alaska). The past couple of years, I have used meat baits sparingly and have not seen any reduction in the number or size of the bears I draw in.

Sweets

I must be related to black bears. We certainly have the same sweet tooth. Black bears love sweets, and once they find a bait that is replenished with sweet stuff, they'll often move in and live there. Old doughnuts and pastries are the best if you can get them in large enough quantities from your local grocery store or doughnut shop.

Black bears love kibbled dog food. I like to pour some out, then dump some sweet pancake syrup on it for added attraction.

If not, you can do some other things. A staple bait for me is kibble-type dog food, which is inexpensive and goes a long way, covered with a lot of pancake syrup.

Bread, table scraps and other filler-type foods covered with syrup are also good. Bears love peanut butter too, if you can get enough of it, as well as jams and jellies. A friend uses a mixture of grain, brown sugar and water, which he mixes in a barrel and lets ferment a little. Bears are not teetotalers, I assure you!

Once you get into baiting, you'll find that different bears prefer different foods. That's why initially I like to give them a bit of everything. I will dump a hundred pounds of dog food into my barrel and soak it with syrup. On top, I'll place all the doughnuts I can get my hands on. As part of a nearby ground set, I'll include meat scraps or salmon heads. This gives the bears a choice. When they find something they like, they're more likely to hang around.

That's exactly what we want.

Clean Up Your Act

As the saying goes, the job isn't over until the paperwork is done. Translated into bear baiting terms, this means the hunt isn't over until you've cleaned up your bait site.

Once I am done hunting a specific bait site, I am meticulous about cleaning it up. I take as much time as needed to scour the area, removing everything. That includes any residual paper or plastic from bait packaging I may have used, the barrel if I have used a barrel and not a ground set, my treestand, and any other unnatural objects I may have brought to the party.

If there is leftover bait, I either dig a hole and bury it, or shove it up under some brush. Sure, other critters—and probably other bears—will eat it up, but I want to get it out of the way. I sometimes bring a shovel and rake to manicure the site; I try to leave it as natural-looking as possible. Lastly, I remove my bait station permit and sign. If I flagged the trail to the bait, I take all the flagging down on my way out.

In most states, such a cleanup procedure is the law. Even if it weren't, it's the right thing to do. Ethical hunters respect both the land and the other people who may pass through the area later. I try to leave as little in the way of human sign in the woods as possible. You should too.

Bear baiters must return the woods to their natural state once the season is over. Be sure to haul out all your garbage and other non-natural objects you may have brought into the forest.

ESTABLISHING A NEW BAIT STATION

When I first started baiting bears, I didn't have a clue. I had just moved to an area of coastal Alaska that is, as they say, a bear-rich environment. How tough could it be?

All I had to do was find a little spot that was easy to access and out of the way so others wouldn't stumble on to it, throw down some meat, hang a treestand, and try to be patient as I waded through the many different bears I was sure would be fighting among themselves for the privilege of living at my bait.

I was in for a rude awakening. My friend Bill and I decided we'd partner up, so we set about trying some new spots. Of course there was head-deep snow everywhere when we began our search for bait sites in early spring, so we had to break out the snowshoes to tromp around checking some spots out. We first went to areas where either Bill or some other friends had spotted spring bears in years past, then tried some places that just looked good to us. In all, we set up four different stands, sliding barrels in over the snow, trimming trees, setting treestands, and gathering bait. Baiting bears, I learned quickly, is hard work.

Of those four stands, only one of them proved to be any good. Of the other three, two never did

Baiting begins in early spring, when there is still lots of snow on the ground and accessing bait sites is a lot of hard work! It often takes trying several potential new bait sites before you find one that's a "keeper."

see any bear action, and one saw only minimal action from small bears. The fourth stand, however, was a gem. We took a large boar off that spot every year for five years.

Since then we've tried several new spots, all of which have turned out to be good ones. Some, of course, prove to be better than others. We've learned that choosing a spot for a bait station is more than randomly going out and throwing some goodies down. You must have a reason for choosing a spot, and once committed, be ready, willing and able to work long and hard at making it a success. Here are some strategies for success.

Start Before the Season

One thing you will quickly learn about bear baiting is that it takes massive quantities of bait to do the job right. If you run more than one station at a time, the amount of bait you need increases exponentially. It isn't unusual for just a single bait station to gobble up a thousand pounds or more of bait per season!

Some bait, like kibbled dog food, you can buy relatively cheaply as you need it. Some you can pick up as the need arises. However, it is wise to line up sources of bait *and* start collecting bait yourself well before the spring hunting season.

Go to your local grocery store or meat market and speak with the butcher. Ask about obtaining meat trimmings. You'd think this would be a no-brainer; after all, they just toss it out, right? But others are interested in it too. There are other bear baiters, as well as folks who collect it to feed to their dogs. I know one woman who likes to feed

Serious baiters collect bear bait during the off-season and store it in an old freezer. When it is time to begin setting baits, these guys have hundreds of pounds of prime bait right from the start.

Plastic 5-gallon pails are perfect for hauling bait into the woods. They are rugged, and they keep the mess off the bed of your truck.

raptors with beef trim and bones.

Day-old doughnuts are also in high demand. Every bear baiter in the country wants them. Some bakers donate them to homeless shelters, some to senior citizen homes. A local fast-food restaurant may sell day-old fryer grease to a recycling company rather than toss it out. The point is that you need to line up your sources of bait in winter, well ahead of spring bear season.

If you are really serious, you'll buy an old freezer and dedicate it for bait storage in the off-season. Meat scraps and trimmings, old doughnuts, and so on, can all be frozen so you can stockpile bait until it's time to hunt. The same is true with your own prime household table scraps. Meat trim, ham bones and other fatty meat byproducts are worth saving. So is bacon grease. Bears may at times be finicky about what they eat, but I have yet to see a black bear that did not go out of his way to get to a jug of bacon grease.

Other than gathering bait, make sure you have: a treestand in good working order; all the basic, essential hunting gear one needs for a bear hunt; and a trail timer that will tell you when bears visit your bait site. (For more on trail timers, see page 64.)

In spring, black bears begin roaming in search of food as soon as they emerge from their dens. Locate your bait stands in traditional bear travel corridors and you will tremendously increase your odds for success.

PICK A SPOT

Success in any hunting endeavor—whether hunting elk, whitetails, sheep or bears—is dependent on what I call the real estate principle—location, location, location. You can't take a good animal unless there are good animals in the area. To find those prime locations, you have to do your homework.

Let's assume you already know that baiting is legal in the state or province you want to hunt, and that it is legal for you as a nonresident to hunt black bears on your own and use bait. (The state-by-state bear summary in Chapter 10 will help here.) As you begin researching more specific areas to hunt, check for any local regulations on baiting. Even in states where baiting is legal, there may be areas governed by local ordinances that prohibit baiting. A common example is baiting near a dump.

Choosing a location for hunting is a process I call "shrink your focus." Your initial focus is on hunting black bears over bait, so you pick a state that permits baiting. Then you need to shrink

your focus down from the entire state to a portion of that state, then smaller to a specific area within that smaller portion.

You do this by talking with people. Call state or province game biologists and ask questions. Where are the highest bear densities in the state? Where are the largest bears? Are there harvest statistics that show hunter success rates and the age and sex of the bears being taken? This information leads to more telephone (or Internet) time.

Once you narrow the area to the region near a specific town, ask local fish and game officials, wildlife protection officers, taxidermists, and anyone else you can think of, where they would recommend you try. Most states that permit baiting require hunters to register their bait stations with the state, which makes this information available to you in your research.

When Bill and I first started out, we had one thing right. We tried setting baits in areas where others had seen bears in the spring. If bears naturally use an area as a travel corridor, it just makes sense that this would be a good place to set a bait station.

Once you've narrowed your focus, there is nothing left to do except walk the ground. Bear baiting is so much easier for local residents simply because they can walk the ground and scout

Topographic maps will help you pre-select potential new bait sites. Look for lowland swamps, tree edges, creeks and other natural bear funnels. The next step: Simply walk the ground to check it out.

I've had my best luck setting bait stations near moving water. Black bears like water, and the creek noise helps mask human sounds from their sharp ears.

much more easily than traveling hunters. Be that as it may, when scouting for a potential place to set a bait station, look for the following:

1. There must be a dependable natural spring food source nearby. This can be many things. In coastal Alaska and British Columbia, salmon streams draw bears like magnets later in summer, and there are always bears around them early. In parts of the Pacific Northwest, bears love manzanita berries, so setting up baits near manzanita thickets makes sense. In the Southwest, prickly pear cactus is a favored food. In areas where fruit orchards abound, you can be sure bears will be close by. Hillsides that grow the spring's first lush grasses following winter snows, and also favorite plants, like skunk cabbage, are great places to search for bears. A local fish and game biologist can help you identify these foods.

2. There must be a water source close to the bait. Bears need lots of water to drink, and water helps grow many of the foods these opportunistic feed-

ers prefer. Also, water helps keep bears cool in hot weather. Water sources such as creek channels, streambeds and lake or pond edges are all natural game-movement funnels. Everything moves along their edges, including bears. I try to set my baits right on a small creek or stream, on a beaver pond or along the edge of a swamp. My bait is never more than a quarter mile from a dependable water source.

3. Never set a bait close to an area hunted by houndsmen. If there are hound hunters in your area, try to find out where they like to hunt. The last thing you need to do is draw in bears only to have them run off by a pack of dogs.

4. Try to set up your bait on the tops of ridges, as opposed to the bases of hills. This makes it easier to get above a bear's line of sight and, most importantly, above its line of smell. These areas are also natural pathways for bears to walk along.

5. East-facing slopes are preferable to west-facing slopes. That's because the east-facing slopes are in the shade earlier in the evening, giving the bears more time to come to the bait during legal shooting hours.

6. Make sure the bait is set up in thick cover. Black bears, by their very nature, are secretive animals that prefer to move under the cover of dark-

Make sure there is a reliable water source in your bait site area. Bears and water go hand-in-hand.

Make your bait setup in thick cover, where bears might venture while there's still shooting light.

ness. They also keep to thick cover. Many first-time bear baiters are unaware that bears are watching them as they set their baits in open areas of the woods. Consequently, the inexperienced baiters are surprised when they don't see any bears, even though the bait is constantly being hit. That's because the bears come in under the cover of darkness. My own baits are set in extremely thick cover, where I have a clear shooting lane to the bait itself and maybe one other location near the bait. Other than that, I can only see small spots of ground through the thick brush.

BAIT SETUP

I set all my baits for bow shots, setting the treestand or bluff-top ground blind between 20 and 30 yards from the bait. Closer is too close for fidgety bears, farther makes the shot iffy. I try to set treestands at least 20 feet high to make it easier for me to see down into the thick cover and get my scent as high as possible. Treestands should be set in trees that afford lots of background cover, like evergreens, or in clusters of other trees to help hide your outline from the often-underrated eyes of a bear.

When I use a 55-gallon barrel to hold bait, I wire it to the tree so the bears can't drag it off. The hole in which they can reach the food is half the size of the barrel top, large enough so the bears can reach in and paw the food out, but too small for them to stick their heads in. For ground sets I place bait under a root jam or an old log, or dig a small hole before placing the bait. Then I cover it with heavy logs and brush. I want to keep

When setting a stand for a bow shot, set up so that the bruin will have to give you a broadside or quartering-away angle as he approaches the bait itself. Use downed logs to create a man-made "funnel."

other small animals and birds out, and make the bears work to get to the food.

The secret is to erect a system of barriers that makes the bear approach the bait the way you want him to. By using downed logs, cut brush, rocks and natural barriers, you can funnel the bear into the bait so he is either broadside or slightly quartering away from you as he reaches in for a snack. This way, he presents the perfect shot opportunity while not looking in your direction. Always make sure the bait has a large, immobile backstop, like a large tree or rock, that prevents the bear from coming in the back door.

I always use a trail timer at my bait sites. When a bear breaks the beam of light between it and the bait, it records the date and time of the passage. This information is invaluable for learning the time of day the bears are coming to your bait. When the trail timer records dozens (or hundreds, as has been the case in the past) of passings in a single day, you know you have a bear living at your bait. It's time to hunt him.

I like to set my treestands, trim brush, and do all other ground prep work before ever placing any bait on the ground. ATVs are a great way to haul bait barrels, stands and other materials into the woods.

SCENT & SIGHT CONTROL

ait hunters must be extremely conscious of both their scent and their presence in stands where bears can easily see them. Failure to guard against being smelled or seen will guarantee you a season of frustration.

The common myth is that bears have poor eyesight, so you do not need to be worried about being seen. Balderdash. Most baits are hunted at close range, and at these distances bears can and will see you if you are careless. If they see you,

Three rules to make sure bears won't see or smell you: Wear camouflage (if legal). Hang your stand in cover. Be still. This hunter has followed all three guidelines and is ready for success.

and light gloves.

Second, set your stands in cover so they do not stick out like a sore thumb. Ground blinds need to be built so they blend into the existing terrain, using natural branches and brush and disturbing as little natural cover as possible. Treestands must be set in trees with lots of leaves, like evergreens or leafed-out aspens or poplars. Try to keep other dark trees in the background to help break up your outline. In both cases, set stands where they will be in the evening shade, not the direct sunlight.

Third, keep movement on stand to a minimum. Black bears, and especially mature boars, are very cautious when they approach a bait. They hold back in the shadows, watching, smelling and listening for trouble. Doing the hully-gully in a treestand, making noise like shuffling your feet, ripping the zippers of your pack open and shut, banging metal or coughing ... these are all excellent ways to go bearless.

SMELL NO EVIL

Black bears live in a world of smell. Their noses are extremely keen, and they use them both to find food and to avoid danger. You must minimize human odor at the bait site for consistent success.

Hang your stand in evergreens if possible or in other cover that will break up your silhouette and hide you as much as possible.

they usually will simply melt back into the forest, never to be seen again. There are three things you can do to avoid detection.

HIDE IN PLAIN SIGHT: 3 SECRETS

First, where legal, wear drab or camouflage clothing, not blaze orange. Match your camo pattern to the surrounding foliage. Don't forget to cover your shiny face and hands, which can often be accomplished by wearing a mosquito head net

Once I get my bait station built and stand hung, I try to wear rubber gloves when baiting. I do not want to leave an inordinate amount of my smell around the bait. I also wear either knee-high rubber boots or a pair of standard hunting boots featuring the Gore-Tex Supprescent membrane, a breathable membrane that blocks 100 percent of human odor.

Just as important, I spray myself down with an odor-eliminating spray before walking in, and make sure I wear the same outerwear I will wear on stand. Why? Because while I am trying to reduce the amount of human odor around the bait, I know I cannot possibly eliminate it all. When a bear smells a human at my bait, I want him to smell me, and associate my smell with food. If I have a friend who will be hunting my bait, I get a piece of his clothing and bring it with me to hang near the bait. I also make sure I hang a clean rag in a tree near the bait, and spray it with the brand of mosquito repellant I use. In many areas in spring, sitting over a bait without any bug dope on is about as smart as sitting in a cave full of vampire bats. Again, I want the bear to associate this smell with food.

Does all this work? I think it helps tremendously. Many times I have been able to set up a bait station, sit on stand and observe a bear's every shift. Then I will have a friend go and sit there, and they see nothing. The only difference is they are bringing a new smell to the party.

Lately I have been wearing scent-adsorbing outerwear when sitting my baits. Yes, *adsorb* is right. It means "to take up and hold." The super-quiet Redhead Windstopper Supprescent garments have worked very well for me both when hunting black bears and when sitting on stand, hunting whitetails.

The key is to set up your stands, and then hunt out of them, as if you were hunting the wariest whitetail buck. Just like when hunting a mature buck, if an old boar is your goal, take nothing for granted. Your chances for success will increase exponentially.

Knee-high rubber hunting boots or Gore Supprescent boots will help keep human odor off trails that bears might use when coming to your bait site.

Using a commercial scent-eliminating spray before climbing into your stand is one way you can help combat bear-spooking human odor.

Take a bear's nose very seriously. He uses it often … and well. Ignore this acute sense, and you will have no rug or bear roasts to show for your effort.

Is Baiting Ethical?

*I*n modern society, big game hunting in any form is controversial to some. Why must man continue to hunt and kill wild animals when he no longer needs to? Inside that debate is the issue of certain forms of hunting and the issue of fair chase. In today's society is a small faction of "New Age" outdoor writers and wildlife biologists who may hunt, but almost apologize for doing so. They have their own favorite style of hunting and believe that other styles are wrong, unethical or both. They speak out against baiting bears as an unethical form of hunting. And so the question must be asked: Is bear baiting ethical?

Why Bait Bears?

Hunters bait bears for one simple reason—properly done, it is an extremely effective way to get a controlled shot at a mature bear. This is true for two reasons. First, bears are both predators and giant food processors, constantly on the move as they seek out high-calorie foods that will pile on the fat needed to sustain them through winter. And second, the terrain in which most black bears live—the flat, dense bush country of Canada, the thick coastal forests of Alaska, and the swamplands and forests of the Pacific Northwest, upper Midwest and Northeast—is not conducive to the spot-and-stalk method of hunting. Without baiting, few bears would ever be taken.

One common question is, "If baiting bears is ethical, why isn't baiting elk, or mule deer or moose?" This question overlooks the fact that bears and ungulates have lit-

Some people question whether or not baiting bears is "ethical" or "sporting." Those of us who bait every year know how hard the job is and how it lets us be very selective about the bears we harvest.

tle in common. They live in different habitat. Ungulates have much higher population densities, and these animals can be—and are—effectively hunted by stalking, calling or ambushing. Comparing the baiting of bears to the baiting of ungulates is like comparing apples to oranges.

NUISANCE BEARS

One argument against baiting says that teaching bears to eat "garbage" creates a generation of problem bears that associate human food with dumpsters, ice chests, campgrounds and garbage dumps.

But the data does not support this in areas where bear baiting is illegal. California's Mammoth Lakes, a small eastern Sierra town with a highly-publicized bear problem, is a prime example. Black bears attack residential garbage cans, the dump and campgrounds filled with vacationers who refuse to use bear-proof boxes for food storage. The same is true in national and state park campgrounds and in national forest campgrounds across the country, where bears annually rip the doors off cars to get at the food left inside.

One biologist told me that bear problems are related to the supply of natural food sources. In years when natural foods are abundant, bear problems are low or nonexistent. In years when natural food sources are scarce, bears must seek out alternative foods. The easiest pickings include the garbage or, in many cases, dog and bird food left on patios and in outdoor feeders by careless humans.

Selective harvest is what bear baiting is all about. When you pass up sows, cubs and immature boars, then have a crack at a big, mature boar, you've paid your dues and earned your prize.

SELECTIVE HARVEST

One of the big advantages of bear baiting is that it is a great way to harvest only mature boars, leaving sows and cubs—even mature two-year-old cubs still with the sow but just prior to being kicked out of the nest—for seed. Hunters sitting over baits can identify the sex and relative age of the bears that come in, choosing to take only older males. As is the case with all big game species we hunt, game managers prefer the taking of these males from the population.

But game department harvest statistics show that bait hunters do not primarily harvest mature boars. In Alaska, for example, in some areas where baiting has increased, game managers have seen a decrease in the average skull size of all bears being taken, an indication that young bears are being taken over baits. In Idaho and Colorado, game managers have noted that baiters have taken the same percentage of female bears as have spot-and-stalk hunters.

One argument against baiting says it teaches them to be "garbage bears," thus creating a problem with bears invading dumps, campgrounds and the like, but research does not support this claim.

The reasons for this are many. First, many bait hunters are first-time bear hunters on guided hunts, left alone on a stand to judge the bears that come to the bait. To the untrained eye, male bears look no different from female bears, so the hunter shoots what is thought to be a "good one" only to find that it really is not. (For more information on this subject, see page 126 in Chapter 8.) And these inexperienced bear hunters may not have the knowledge—or the patience—to carefully look over a bear's hide for subtle rubs that keep the hide from being prime.

However, baiting is the best way to harvest a high percentage of mature boars. Some states, like Alaska, require unguided hunters to take a bear baiting class before they are allowed to register a bait station. A large part of this class teaches the difference between sows and boars, how to field judge a bear, and stresses the importance of letting the females live.

Is Baiting "Fair Chase"?

This is the crux of the debate. Opponents say that bear baiting is really only killing, not hunting. They believe that by taking advantage of a black bear's monstrous appetite, baiters are not following the tenets of fair chase hunting.

To paraphrase a famous general at World War II's Battle of the Bulge when replying to the German demand of surrender, to this I say, "Nuts!"

First off, bear baiting is hard work. I spend many days each spring prepping new bait sites, setting treestands, clearing brush and, once under-

The latest anti-baiting argument calls it a social rather than a biological issue. Bear hunting is one of anti-hunters' targets these days, and hunters should be prepared to defend all forms of bear hunting against these attacks.

way, replenishing bait. Over the years I have backpacked thousands of pounds of bait to my bait stations. Scouting for potential new bait sites is an ongoing endeavor, and many of them never pan out. Those who say that baiting is "easy" have never participated at this level!

Detractors say that baiting is a sure way to kill a bear. They think all you have to do is put out some food, set a stand and shoot a bear—just like that. *Au contraire*. Baiting is anything but a sure thing.

On four separate hunts, I sat for six straight days *each* (that's 24 days total) in good bait locations across Alberta and Saskatchewan ... and never had a crack at a good bear. On the baits I set near my coastal Alaska home, I spent an entire season looking at small bears, rubbed bears, sows with cubs and, occasionally, grizzlies, and never took a shot. In those years, ironically, I took several bears on one-day spot-and-stalk trips.

When talking about taking advantage of a bear's appetite, I ask whether or not taking advantage of an ungulate's sex drive is unsporting. After all, the wariest whitetail or bull elk becomes a relative pushover when the rut has him by the throat. Does that make hunting during the rut unethical? In dry years in hot weather, setting a deer or elk stand over a water hole is pretty much a sure thing. Does that make this unethical? How about hunting deer over food plots planted specifically for that purpose? After all, isn't hunting about taking advantage of a particular game animal's inherent weakness at a particular time?

Social Ramifications

The latest anti-baiting argument calls it a social, not a biological, issue. Across the country, citizens are using "ballot box biology" by passing referendums that outlaw certain forms of hunting that are unacceptable to them, like bear baiting and the use of hounds. They don't care whether baiting has a negative impact on the resource, only the false image that lazy hunters are shooting bears that have their heads stuck in a mound of stale doughnuts.

The anti-baiting initiatives have been the work of known anti-hunting groups, whose goal it is to eliminate any and all forms of sport hunting. These groups have chosen the bear-baiting issue as an early target in a long battle because it is a relatively easy issue for them to attack. After all, black bears are endangered, right? That's why people never see them. And they're so cute. How could you take advantage of such a cuddly creature like that? When put this way—and that's exactly how the anti's portray it—the general non-hunting public, with no knowledge of black bear habits or population numbers, and with no personal stake in the issue, is going to vote to ban baiting.

And yet biologists will tell you that taking black bears over baits has done nothing to negatively impact overall bear populations. These professional game managers are the ones who should dictate how our game resources should be managed, not an uninformed voting block swayed by slick advertising campaigns run by avowed anti-hunting groups.

Is Bear Baiting Ethical?

Because bear baiting has no negative biological impact on what is today a growing black bear population, the only reason to not hunt bears over bait is an ethical one. Ethics are an individual thing. Each of us must decide individually what is right and wrong in the woods.

If hunting bears over baits does not seem like

fair chase to you, so be it. Hunt your bears by spotting, stalking, ambushing or calling them. Personally, I enjoy bear baiting about as much as any form of big game hunting I do. It permits me to spend a lot of time around bears, observing their habits. It allows me to be very selective if and when the time comes to shoot a bear—and often a mature boar never presents himself, even though I know from the sign that one is using a particular bait regularly.

As a fraternity, sport hunters need to stick together when challenged by the anti's on issues like bear baiting. Never forget that their stated goal is to eliminate all forms of hunting, no matter how long it takes. It's the old "united we stand, divided we fall" concept.

Even if you, as an individual, do not hunt black bears over bait, as a group we must respect the tradition of those who choose to hunt bears this way. Letting someone else dictate ethics to us is simply the wrong thing to do. Sticking together will ensure our, and our sons' and daughters', hunting future.

Because bear baiting has not been shown to have any negative biological impact on what is today a growing bear population throughout the animal's range, the only reason not to bait bears is for social or ethical reasons. And in my mind, there is nothing unethical about bear baiting.

Chapter 4

SPOT & STALK BEAR HUNTING

*I*t seemed like a good idea at the time. Mike and I had spotted the bear from the valley floor as he was munching away on some fresh grass. The mountain was steep, the kind most people associate with sheep or mountain goats. Over the years we've found that steep hillsides mean nothing to black bears, though.

So off we went, climbing through patches of thigh-deep snow and pulling our way up with whatever brush we could grab. Halfway up I wondered what we were thinking. Of course, two hours later, when we finally got to the meadow where we had last seen the bear, he was gone.

So we waited, as much to recover as anything. In an hour the bear began feeding again, and before long we were skinning and butchering him. The packs were heavy on the way down, and when we finally reached the truck we were both physically bone-tired and sore. But our spirits were soaring. It had taken a week of afternoon hunts and several fruitless climbs before we finally hit the jackpot.

I truly love spot-and-stalk hunting for all big game, including black bears. Not only is it a very effective way to hunt, it also gives me time to enjoy the vast expanses of the wild country in which this technique is most effective.

Successful spot-and-stalk bear hunting is more than just plopping down someplace and using your binoculars. You have to know where bears are likely to be, and when they are most likely to be there. You have to know what draws them to a certain place, why they walk where they do, and when they are apt to abandon one area for another. You have to have the right equipment and know how to use it properly. And once you've found the bear you want, you have to know how to close the gap without spooking him.

Want to learn more? Then read on ...

Stalking is not still-hunting. A stalk begins once game is spotted and you start sneaking in on the animal. In the case of the black bear, you have a big challenge ahead: to get close enough for a good shot.

Hunting Black Bears

Spot & Stalk Secrets

ost black bears are hunted over baits or on stands sitting over agricultural fields, swamps, orchards and other similar attractants. However, in many areas of the West, as well as across some parts of Canada, spot-and-stalk hunting is the name of the game.

Spot-and-stalk is most closely associated with Western hunters after mule deer, Coues' deer, pronghorn, elk, mountain sheep and similar game found in open and semi-open country where distances are long and the best chances of finding game is to simply plop down in a good spot and seek it out using high-quality optics.

Keep in mind that, by definition, spot-and-stalk hunting is not still-hunting, whereby the hunter is continually slipping through relatively small patches of cover in search for game he's not sure is there. The still-hunter may be confident that he's in good bear country, but he is not actively stalking a particular animal.

Stalking, on the other hand, does not begin until you have located—by spotting—the animal you want to hunt. It is at that time, and not before, that you begin sneaking in, stalking the animal and trying for your shot.

Black bears can be successfully hunted using the spot-and-stalk method. In fact, for the hunter who does his homework and spends time in a good area, it's an excellent way to fill a bear tag. Here are the key advantages of the spot-and-stalk method.

Black bears like to work along edge cover, specifically where trees meet open parks. They can ghost in and out, so be prepared to look long and hard.

Maximum coverage. Spotting is very efficient. In short, you can look over a lot of country from one strategic vantage point, saving your energy and boot leather for the actual stalk. Spotting your bear from far away lets you plan the stalk without spooking him off, and without your scent reaching his incredible nose.

Huntable bears. Spotting allows you to judge how good the stalking opportunity is. If it in fact is a good one, you have time to plan your route and go to work. If the bear is in a bad spot, sit back and wait him out until he moves to a position where you can get at him. If the bear starts moving flat-out, you have to make a decision: let him go, or try to anticipate his route and then head him off.

Pollution-free hunting. Bears are smart.

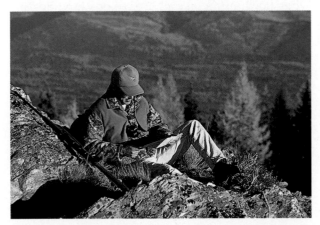

Use a map to find the best vantage points in a piece of country. Then glass, glass, glass … especially in the evening.

Maybe smart isn't the right word, but take the following words seriously: If you tramp around in the best bear country, making noise and being seen and, worst of all, leaving your scent, the bears there are going to become much more difficult to kill. They may go totally nocturnal on you, or they may just vacate the premises altogether. It is better to stay on the fringes of the prime bear country, trying to spot bears, and then move in only when the opportunity to get a shot is good.

Selection. By spotting, you will have a good opportunity and plenty of time to really evaluate each bear you see and decide whether or not it is one you want to pursue. Maybe you'll spot a cub or two and realize that good-sized bear you're watching is a sow. Maybe you'll take a long look and find some rubs on a boar's hide that give him clemency for this year.

Efficiency. You'll just save a lot of steps on your feet and wear-and-tear on your body when you plop down at a good vantage point and let your eyes do the walking. Even in the very best bear country, only a tiny proportion of the land actually holds a bear, let alone a bear that is out and about looking for food or otherwise traveling. A hike is nice, but you'll find more bears by locating an excellent spotting vantage point and putting your optics and eyes to work.

PRIME-TIME BEARS

One of the most important tools of the spot-and-stalk bear hunter is his flashlight. Say what?

That's because bears are animals that love shadow time, those gray twilight hours around dawn and dusk. To maximize your chances of spotting a bear at these times, you have to be on your glassing station and ready to look before first

Glassing big country is the most efficient way to hunt it. By spending your time looking instead of walking, you'll efficiently cover far more ground.

light, and stay until you cannot see any more. That means hiking in and out by flashlight.

The flashing principle is pretty simple, isn't it? And yet I meet hunters every year who are afraid of the bogeyman, or are scared they'll get lost in the dark, so they are never on station in time. When spotting bears, I'd trade the rest of the day for the first hour and last hour of available light. That's when the most, and biggest, bruins are usually seen.

Given the choice between hunting in the morning or in the evening, most bear hunters will choose the evening. It just seems that you spot more bears in late afternoon and evening than at any other time of day. Generally speaking, I build my hunting days around spotting from supper time until I can't see anymore.

That isn't to say you cannot spot bears at other times too. I've seen many a large black bear feeding at lunch time. On overcast, drizzly and rainy days, bears are apt to be out moving just about any time. As with all hunting, the more hours you spend in the field, the better your chances of success. It's just that when bear hunting—and especially in spring, when the days are almost endless—you do have to sleep sometime. For me that means the mornings are for sleeping in, and then I hunt hard from noon until slap dark.

PLANNING THE STALK

Once you've spotted a bear you want to go after, it's time to plan the stalk. How you go about stalking the bear is determined by two things: the weapon you're hunting with, and what the bear is doing.

Obviously, bowhunters must be much more meticulous in their decisions than firearms hunters. After all, if you spook the bear you want while bowhunting, it's all over. Spook it while carrying a .300 Magnum, and the rifle becomes your eraser, wiping out your mistake with its long-range killing power.

For that reason, when I'm bowhunting, I much prefer to spot a bear as early in the afternoon as I possibly can, try to pattern him as best I can and then get going. Generally speaking, you are going to see bears up feeding, so they are constantly on the move. That makes stalking within bow range very difficult, simply because you never really know what the bear will do next.

When I can, I try to get above the bear, find him, then get ahead of him and let him come to me. This is best done in broken country, where folds in the land provide natural cover. Stalking

When making a stalk, be sure first to get the wind in your favor, then try to work toward the bear from slightly above him while using trees, rocks and brush for cover.

what about other game—a browsing deer, grazing elk or wandering caribou perhaps? What about coyotes or maybe even wolves? And don't forget all the other wildlife that shares the countryside with bears. Know where these animals are, and watch out for them as you plan and then make your approach.

Know the land. The more stalks you make, the more you learn this essential point: The countryside always looks really different when you're in the middle of it, compared to what it appeared to be back at your spotting vantage point! What can you do? Study the lay of the land very carefully before you set off. I like to carry a small notebook and pen, and draw a basic map before I begin a stalk. I'll mark where the bear is, its likely movement path, the position of any other animals, and prominent landmarks such as lone or big trees, large and distinctive boulders, gullies and so forth. It sounds sort of goofy, but it works.

Use hand signals. If you have a hunting buddy with you, your chances of making a successful stalk go up exponentially if one of you stays back at the spotting point and gives hand signals as the other moves in. Of course, this requires that the two of you communicate clearly on what each hand signal means—your position

from below is really hard to do. The bottom line: You have to evaluate each situation as it comes, then make a "go" or "no go" decision based upon what's happening at that moment.

No matter what, I follow the same basic game plan when planning a stalk with a rifle, handgun or muzzleloader as I do when bowhunting. That is, I want to get within comfortable shooting range of an undisturbed bear. The long-range capabilities of firearms makes those stalks a much easier proposition, of course. My basic step-by-step program when planning a stalk goes something like this:

Get the whole picture. Before you take off after the bear, take control of your emotions for just one minute and assess the situation. Is there more than one bear? That might put a wrench in your stalk plan. How are you going to keep the sun at your back and the wind in your face? What are the best terrain features—draws, creekbottoms, timber stringers, brush, rock piles—that you can use for cover as you work toward the bear?

Ask: Is there other game in the picture? We've mentioned looking for other bears. But

Stalking a moving bear in semi-open country is difficult, as the bear will almost always be moving to feed when you see him. Get ahead of him, set up, and find him again before moving in for a shot.

Patience is a virtue when stalking bears. When you get close, stay behind a screen of cover to keep him from picking you up.

in relation to the bear (is he above, below, in front of or behind you), how far he is, what his movement is, and a wave-off if the bear spooks and goes. The stalker should use binoculars to look back at the signaler often, and the signaler should wear an orange hat or vest to be easily located.

Be patient. I love bear hunting, and when I spot a good bruin my initial instinct is to rush over and shoot him *now*!

But that's not the best plan, and I've learned to control my emotions. You should too. Be patient. Make your move only when the time is right. If you get to where you think the bear should be and he's not, don't give up in a huff. Rather, sit down and wait awhile, from a nice vantage point if you can get there silently. Bears will often lie down for awhile and get up to feed again after a short nap. I've shot more than one bear this way!

GETTING THE SHOT

There are some things you need to do as you close in on the bear, to make sure your "spot-and-stalk" hunt doesn't become a "spot-and-spook"

Use your binoculars to relocate the bear when you get close. It is amazing how easily a big, furry black bear can disappear in the brush!

affair. The whole idea is to move in undetected for a good shot at an unsuspecting and undisturbed animal. Here are some tips.

Always relocate the bear. If he was feeding in thick cover, or bedded in a good hiding spot, or you had to dip behind some terrain features as you made your approach ... don't just go barging on in. Whether you're hunting with rifle, handgun, or bow, this is the make-or-break point of your stalk.

Use your binoculars to find the bear again. This is true even if the quarters are close and the distance between you and the bear is relatively short. Look for pieces of a bear—a glossy black nose, a shimmering eye, a flicking ear, a horizontal back or belly line in a sea of vertical brush—rather than a whole bear.

Peek up and over rises, around tree trunks or grass clumps or boulders, under boughs and limbs. Be sneaky. Even though that bear was very visible from your spotting point, you're in his territory now and it looks a lot different here. So don't give up. Be patient. Don't stand up and blow it now!

That bear may have fed off a ways, but he will still be relatively close by unless he panicked and quit the country. My rule of thumb is this: Unless I actually saw the bear run off, he's still there. Somewhere. So I keep sneaking and looking, patiently working until I find him again.

HANG LOOSE

Spot-and-stalk hunting is both exciting and fun. No two opportunities are ever the same, which is one reason the most successful spot-and-stalk bear hunters are those who have spent a lot of time in the woods. They know where the bears like to hang out, what they like to eat during both spring and fall, and where they like to walk. These hunters have scouted and found bear scat, rootings and other bear sign. They have quality optics and know how to use them.

Most of all, though, they know how to go with the flow, adapting both their hunting method and the pace of a particular day's hunt to the conditions at hand. When hunting bears this way, there's a time to go slow and a time to run. You have to be able to read the conditions, and be ready to do whatever it takes to get the shot.

It is a grand adventure.

FINDING BEARS

Spot-and-stalk hunting is an excellent method because it permits you to look at a lot of country as you search for bears. By accessing a good vantage point, then glassing miles of country, you cover the maximum amount of territory with minimal effort.

However, you can sit for days and never see a bear unless you are in the right area. As discussed earlier, the secret is to do your homework and find areas that bears frequent, then spend your time there, not in some place where you think there might be a bear.

Black bears do not necessarily frequent the same location in both spring and fall. Also, even though they might use the same mountainside for travel during the entire year, conditions can change and make locating and hunting them impractical.

A good example is the huge mountains in coastal areas of Alaska. In early spring, the snow is melting and the bears are starting to come out of their dens. Alders and other brush are just starting to spring back from being buried under the snow, and have neither grown to maximum size—they will grow much taller than a man—nor leafed out yet.

Prime time for spring spot-and-stalk hunting in this region is a window of two to four weeks just after the bears have emerged, but before the alders and brush have grown tall and are thickly leafed out. Once this occurs, it is so thick that spotting the bears becomes extremely difficult. If you do spot a bear, climbing up through this horrible brush is almost impossible. If you make it through the brush to the area where you last saw the bear, it's likely that the bear has moved along; relocating it in this jungle

To put yourself in this position—ready to take a shot at a mature black bear—you have to be able to locate one first. That means understanding how they live, where they live, and what they eat at different times of the year.

is like trying to find a four-leaf clover.

In fall, there are different problems, but these generally revolve around food. As we have seen, black bears have preferred food sources that will draw and hold them as long as the food holds out. Once that food source has been depleted, the bears will move on in search of the next gourmet meal. You must be hunting these food sources while there is enough to attract and sustain them, not before or after.

Berry patches are a prime example. If the huckleberry crop is a good one and there are bears in the area, you can bet your bottom dollar that they will be there gobbling up the goodies. But before the berries ripen and after the bulk of the berries are gone, the bears will be off looking for something else to eat. Again, timing is everything.

SPRING SPOTTING

In mountainous country, I have had good success glassing mountainsides where I know bears are denning. You have to access denning areas early, often before all the snow is gone, which makes getting into prime territory problematic at times. The goal is to locate bears that have just emerged from their dens, before they take off for prime spring food sources. Often bears will hang around a den for a few days, and this is when the finest, lushest hides can be had.

As spring progresses, you have to hunt food sources. In spring, bears key on vegetation. Studies show that plant matter makes up more than 90 percent of their diet at this time. Succulent green grasses and new shrubs, and plants with edible roots—like wild onions, skunk cabbage and glacier lilies—are favored. You can find these plants on

Swampy bottoms, creeks, and stream and lake edges ... all are bear magnets in spring as the animals seek new-growth plants and water.

mountainside avalanche chutes, old burns, clear cuts, meadows, beaches and along power lines and ditches.

In areas with lots of snow, the bears will follow the snow line up and down the mountain. In early spring, bears tend to be high, feeding in small open patches. Then as the snow level begins to recede back up the mountain from bottom to top, they will drop down low and follow the melt line back up. That's because as the snow melts, new plants spring forth—and that's just what bears are looking for.

In flatland areas, hunt the swampy bottoms, hollows, along creeks, and stream and lake edges for newly emerging plants, and the edges of farmland where bears might find crops springing forth.

Also, be aware that as the spring progresses from May into June, the breeding urge begins to play a role in bear behavior. Boars will begin cruising for sows in heat, covering lots of territory. If I have found an area where there is a sow with a couple two-year-old cubs, the chances are very good that she will be kicking those cubs out soon and be ready to breed again this year. It makes sense to keep watching her; when she does come into heat, the chances are very good there will be a boar moving in.

When bears first emerge from their dens in spring, they are ravenous, roaming far and wide in search of food. Find the food and you will find the bears.

Hunting Black Bears

In fall, food sources are again the key to locating black bears. Berries, mast crops and fruit are their three favorites this time of year, together with agricultural crops in farmland areas.

FALL SPOTTING

In fall, food sources are paramount to success. Always look for the "big three" food sources—berries, mast crops and fruit—as well as spawning salmon in Alaska, British Columbia and parts of the Pacific Northwest.

Find out what bears prefer to eat in the area you will be hunting. In the mountains, huckleberry patches found on north-facing slopes draw bears from miles. Manzanita berries, blueberries, blackberries and other foods of this type draw them like flies too. In the Southwest, prickly pear patches and scrub oaks are bear magnets. In the East, beechnuts and acorns are prime-time bear food, as are fruit orchards. And wherever they can find it, crop fields filled with corn, soybeans, wheat, and the like, cannot be resisted.

An example of crop field hunting occurs in portions of the Carolinas, where hunters often position their treestands overlooking cornfields. The stands are set after scouting to locate fresh bear sign—tracks, scat and sign of active feeding in the fields themselves. Hunters wait on stand to ambush the bears as they enter the fields, usually during late afternoon and evening hours.

WATCH THE WIND

It is critical to play the wind when spotting and stalking bears. If the wind is wrong, forget about it. When spotting and/or still-hunting in "enclosed" areas like the hardwood forests east of the Mississippi River, swamp country and overgrown clear cuts, always begin your approach from downwind of the "core" area in which you expect to find bears.

In this tight cover, I am a believer in using the same fanatical scent-control system I use when whitetail hunting from a treestand. That includes showering with unscented soap and shampoo, laundering my clothes in unscented detergent, using unscented deodorant and/or body gel, and wearing either under- or outerwear and footwear featuring a scent-adsorbing agent.

For clothing and footwear, my personal favorite is Gore's Supprescent fabric, which breathes yet blocks 100 percent of my scent. Scent-Lok and Robinson Labs' Scent-Blocker are other popular clothing products of this type.

Even in the mountains, where you'll generally spot the bears from a long distance, you have to be scent conscious and play the wind. Never trust a mountain wind! It can bounce off trees, mountainsides, lakes, boulders and other objects that cause it to swirl and dance unpredictably.

Always monitor the wind with some sort of easily-seen device. The flame from a butane lighter works, as does a small "puff bottle" filled with unscented talc, cornstarch or powdered carpenter's chalk. Windfloaters are my favorite, as these ultra-light pieces of kapok float on the slightest breeze, and can be seen from a long distance, helping you scope out the exact way the wind is working from wherever you are standing.

Constantly monitoring the wind when bear hunting is critical to success. A puff bottle can help you do this.

When stalking a feeding bear, I like to circle around whenever possible and get behind the hill he is on, staying just below the crest. Then when I get close to where he is, I will slip over the top, relocate the bear and make my move. By putting the hill between us, I have greatly reduced the chances that he will smell, see or hear me.

EQUIPMENT CHOICES

Above and beyond all else, serious spot-and-stalk bear hunting is a game of glassing. Consistently successful hunters know that the best way to find a bear is to access good bear country, find a good vantage point, plop down and glass for hours. To that end, more than just about any other equipment choice—including everything from your rifle or bow to your boots—choosing the right pair of binoculars is the most important selection you'll ever make.

Consistently successful spot-and-stalk hunters know that their success depends on quality optics. Buy the best binoculars you can afford, with 8X to 10X magnification. They must be both waterproof and fogproof.

When glassing broken terrain for bears, pick a good vantage point, get comfortable, and glass the edges long and hard. A big ball of black fur can hide in places where you'd think he would stick out like a sore thumb! Evenings are statistically your best chance for spotting feeding bears.

KEY HUNTING BINOCULAR FEATURES

There are several key features that make up top-of-the-line hunting binoculars. When comparing brands A and B, use these features as your benchmark.

Light-gathering ability. In hunting situations, the more ability binoculars have to gather and utilize available light, the better. This is critical very early and late in the day, when bears are most active. Generally speaking, the larger the objective lens, the more light will be transmitted to your eye. For example, 10X50 binoculars will deliver more light than 10X28. To compare binoculars on an even scale, simply divide the size of the objective lens by the magnification to get the "twilight factor." For example, a pair of 10X50 binoculars has a twilight factor of 5.0, while 8X30 binoculars have a twilight factor of 3.75.

Lens coatings. Light tends to reflect off glass, and by the time it has bounced off the multiple surfaces of a modern-day pair of binoculars, as much as half of the light that initially entered the system may have bounced back out. (There are many more lenses and glass surfaces inside a pair of binoculars than just the objective and ocular lenses.) This could severely reduce the brightness and image quality if it weren't for the chemical coatings on the lenses designed to reduce reflection. All quality binoculars have at least some coatings, but do not necessarily have a coating on all internal surfaces. Top-of-the-line binoculars have high-tech coatings on all lens surfaces, a big reason high-end binoculars cost so much.

Clarity. You must be able to see distant objects clearly, with no eyestrain. If objects appear blurry or your eyes feel tired after looking through the binoculars, they aren't the ones for you.

Waterproof, fogproof. Hunting binoculars must be guaranteed 100 percent waterproof and fogproof. Years ago, this was found only in the most expensive glasses, but today most manufacturers guarantee their products from the mid-price range and up. Avoid products without this assurance.

Handy when bear hunting, a spotting scope will help you judge hide quality and see if there are any tiny newborn cubs nearby, indicating that you don't want to pursue this bear.

How Much Power Is Too Much?

Decades ago, the experts preached that low-power binoculars in the 6X to 7X range were the ideal choice. Today, the biggest sellers are 10X binoculars. However, low-power binoculars have their place too. When still-hunting or sitting a stand in tight cover, for example, low-power binoculars with a wider field of view are a definite advantage. Generally speaking, though, for bear hunting the minimum power to consider is 8X, with 10X my own preferred "all-around" choice.

Serious bear hunters pack a top-quality spotting scope to evaluate hides for rubs at long range. A good spotter can save you hours of time and miles of walking, and should be a standard part of your equipment.

Spotting scopes have to gather enough light to allow you to see in dim light, and be light and compact enough to pack up a mountain, be rugged enough to take some field abuse plus be powerful enough to

permit evaluation of the bear's sex (boar or sow) and coat at a mile or more.

I prefer variable-power spotting scopes, with eyepieces in the 15-45X and 20-60X class. For many years, I've carried Bausch & Lomb's Elite 15-45X spotter with 60mm objective lens, as well as their 20-60X model with 70mm objective lens. These scopes have excellent optics and can really take a pounding in the field.

I've also used spotting scopes from Leupold, Redfield, Burris, Simmons, Fujinon and Nikon with good results. Expect to pay between $450 and $700 for a good spotting scope of this type. Leica and Swarovski make Cadillac-quality spotting scopes, but they cost more than $1,000 and are relatively big and bulky.

You need a good tripod with a spotting scope. I've yet to find a manufacturer that provides a satisfactory one with the scope. Instead, buy a lightweight camera tripod. Get one that extends high enough so that you can sit—not lie—down comfortably behind it without craning your neck. They'll weigh maybe a pound, and cost you around $50.

Pack Essentials

Bear hunters need large-volume, well-designed packs, not the small fanny or teardrop packs treestand whitetail hunters commonly carry. Why? Because in addition to regular, everyday hunting

In his pack, a well-equipped bear hunter carries the tools needed to skin his bear and care for the meat, as well as standard hunting and survival gear.

Depending on where and when you are stalking bears, you can experience everything from hot and dry to cold and wet weather. Wearing the proper clothing system is paramount to remaining at peak efficiency, thereby upping your odds for success.

stuff, and depending on the time of year, black bear hunters need to carry an assortment of bulky gear that includes a rain suit, warm jacket, hat, gloves, lunch, water, spotting scope, field-dressing and skinning gear, and more. And you'll likely be carrying your pack over many miles of broken country. If it's not comfortable to carry, you'll be miserable and less efficient than you would otherwise be.

THE PACK

A top-notch hunting daypack will feature an outer shell material of either polar fleece or one of the new soft nylon fabrics like Stealth Cloth or Saddle Cloth that are whisper-quiet when going through brush.

The pack will also have large, adjustable shoulder straps to help evenly distribute weight, an easily adjustable and well-padded waist belt and chest strap that both feature quick-detach buckles

of high-impact plastic, side pockets large enough for water bottle and spotting scope, plus smaller pockets for lesser items. Some top-quality packs feature a leather or reinforced bottom pad to guard against wear and tear. A waterproof liner inside the main compartment is good.

When hunting bears, I like to carry a full-size frame pack; both internal- and external-frame models are good. With a frame pack, I can carry my day-hunt equipment (even enough equipment to set up a spike camp if need be) and then, if I get a bear, I can pack out the boned-out meat, hide and skull without having to make another trip. Good internal frame packs made by Eureka! and Badlands are perfect for this and have lots of room, are lightweight and have outer shells made from quiet materials. Full-size external frame packs are by far the best for hauling heavy meat loads. The Coleman Freighter frame is the basis for some superb packs of this type.

DRESS FOR SUCCESS

Depending on where and when you're spot-and-stalk hunting bears, you can experience everything from very hot and dry to cold and rainy weather. To remain comfortable and safe, and to be able to hunt at peak efficiency, you have to dress properly.

The key is to view your hunting clothing as a system, not as several different pieces that are entities unto themselves. In this system, all the parts must work together to provide a micro-climate that protects the body from the elements, keeping it warm but not hot, cool but not cold. To be most effective, your garments must be designed for the conditions at hand.

THE IMPORTANCE OF LAYERING

Rather than wear one heavy jacket over a thin shirt, wear several thinner garments that can be removed and/or vented when you're on the move, then put back on or closed up when you're inactive and cold.

For example, hiking up a steep mountainside to get into spotting position will make your body hot, so you need layers on top that can be either removed and carried, or zipped open or unbuttoned to allow body heat to escape. Once you're on top of the mountain, you can add layers as you settle in to glass and your body begins to cool down after the climb.

Initial layers should be a wicking-type synthetic underwear of Thermax, Coolmax or another high-tech fabric that both insulates and wicks moisture—sweat—off the body. Removing this moisture is the key to staying comfortable, one reason cotton undergarments—which lose their insulative values when wet—are a no-no.

OUTERWEAR

Subsequent layers should be made of breathable materials that continue to permit moisture vapor to escape the clothing. Wool and synthetic materials like polar fleece will do this. Your outerwear must protect you from the elements and from brush, rocks and so on, and it must be quiet. That's one reason smart bear hunters never wear scratchy nylon or denim but instead select fleece, wool, or synthetics with a soft hand.

Two breathable high-tech materials that also block 100 percent of the wind and are laminated to many different outerwear shell fabrics are Gore-Tex and Windstopper. Gore-Tex is also 100 percent

Because it is silent when swished by twigs or brush, fleece is a "must" for spot-and-stalk outerwear. Wool is a good, "naturally" quiet alternative.

waterproof, and can be found in not only superb lightweight, packable rain suits from companies like Whitewater Outdoors, Browning, and 10X, among others, but also pants, jackets, gloves, caps and hunting boots. Windstopper is designed for active hiking. I've found that wearing lightweight Windstopper shirts, gloves and caps allows me to actually wear several layers less than in the "old days," before this laminate became available. That translates into less weight and bulk and, as a result, a more efficient hunter.

SCENT-BLOCKING GARMENTS

Black bears have superb noses. One whiff of human scent, and that's it—it's all over. For that reason, I have begun incorporating scent-adsorbing garments into my bear hunting clothing system.

Contemporary scent-blocking garments employ activated carbon (charcoal), which adsorbs (defined by Webster's as "to take up and hold") human scent and prevents these odors from reaching game. Both underwear—worn under your regular hunting outerwear, which ideally has been freshly laundered in no-scent laundry detergent—and outerwear are available. The latest outerwear garments feature an outer shell of quiet, soft synthetic cloth, making it ideal even for close-range hunting, like bowhunting.

Scent-blocking garments for hunting were pioneered by Scent-Lok. The best I've used, however, is W.L. Gore's Supprescent, which imbeds the activated carbon into the company's Windstopper membrane. The end result is high-performance outerwear that blocks human scent and 100 percent of the wind, yet is highly breathable, thereby reducing the number of necessary layers. Whitewater Outdoors, Browning, Redhead (Bass Pro Shops) and 10X all produce Supprescent garments suitable for all big game hunting.

EXTREMITIES

Spot-and-stalk hunting is an active game involving lots of hiking. You need boots that are rugged enough both to offer ankle support and to withstand the abuse of the toughest terrain, yet can breathe and remain waterproof. Gore-Tex boots with an aggressive bob-type sole are the finest all-around all-season hunting boot of this type ever made, offering breathability, waterproofness and toughness. Companies like Danner, Georgia Boot, Wolverine, Rocky Boots and Northlake, among others, build excellent boots of this type. During early bow seasons some archers prefer lightweight canvas shoes or low-cut boots.

The body loses more heat from the head than any other place. Don't overlook protecting both the head and hands. Carrying a stocking cap and pair of lightweight gloves in your pack will allow you to stay warm while glassing from high atop a windy ridge.

Bowhunters need camouflage that blends into surrounding foliage. Wearing a modern scent-adsorbing suit and footwear, like those featuring W.L. Gore's Supprescent membrane, will help tip the odds in your favor.

Rugged, waterproof, breathable footwear is essential for forms of spot-and-stalk hunting. An aggressive bob-type tread (left) is best for steep country, while a less aggressive, self-cleaning tread (right) is best for flatland work.

Chapter 5

SOUND OF THE HOUNDS

On a cold, dreary, sleety October day in western Oregon, houndsman Dave Handrich stood on the edge of a sheer canyon wall, straining to hear something. "There," he whispered. "That's ol' Blue on a bear. Doesn't he sound wonderful?"

Soon I could hear ol' Blue along with two more of Dave's dogs. It was a primal sound, one that hunters have been following for thousands of years. Once a skeptic of hound hunting, I gained an immediate appreciation for Handrich and others like him. I was hooked too.

Anti-hunters call the use of hounds to pursue and bay up game—like bears and mountain lions—inhumane and unsporting. Anti's also say that houndsmen are cruel to their dogs and have little or no respect for the land and its wildlife.

In fact, by trailing hounds on foot over some of the West's most difficult terrain, these men and women have learned more about the country they love and respect, and about the animals that live there, than anyone else I know. They love and respect their dogs and care for them attentively.

And are hound hunts unsporting? Hardly. Some of the most physically demanding hunting trips I have ever been on involved following hounds up, down and all around some of the steepest mountains there are, in rain, sleet and snow, trying to catch up to the dogs and a bear. It has been exhilarating, exhausting and many times frustrating. Those times when a bear was taken, I have felt real pride and accomplishment. Many times after racing to a tree or rocky bluff where the dogs have a bear bayed up, I've let the bear walk for several reasons— its hide was rubbed, the bear was too small or it was a sow.

If you've never run to the sound of the hounds, you are missing one of hunting's great experiences. Come along as we run back in time and follow a sound sure to penetrate your very soul.

BEAR DOG BASICS

There are few houndsmen left today who run bear dogs for their own pleasure. Most hound hunters are guides and outfitters who take clients in pursuit of bears, mountain lions and bobcats.

If you are considering a black bear hunt with hounds, chances are you'll hire an experienced guide who has his own pack of trained dogs. It will be your job to follow along and try to keep up as the hounds take you around some of the country's most rugged areas as you chase a bear. Even though you'll be hunting with someone

The tradition of hunting with hounds dates back hundreds of years. Today it still holds the same primal excitement it did back then. Pursuing black bears with hounds is also a very effective way of harvesting a mature boar.

Most hound hunting is conducted by licensed guides who care for a pack of well-trained hounds year-round. A houndsman may turn loose anywhere from two to a half-dozen or more dogs when a fresh track is cut.

else's hounds, you'll find increased enjoyment if you have a rudimentary knowledge of hunting hounds and what you might expect on your hunt.

BEAR DOGS

Hound hunters use several different breeds of dogs to run bears. The most common are Walkers, Plott hounds, blue ticks, redbones and black-and-tans. Many good hounds are crossbreeds and even have non-hound bred into them, like pit bull or Airedale. Bear hounds usually weigh between 40 and 75 pounds. This size is ideal for giving the dogs the stamina needed to chase bears for long distances, the quickness and agility required to harass the bear at close quarters yet get out of the way when things begin to get interesting.

A good hound will have a loud, deep, throaty voice that can be heard from a long distance, enabling the hunters to follow him to the tree the bear has climbed.

Most dog packs are comprised of three to six dogs, or sometimes more. Houndsmen will often include a young, inexperienced dog or two with their better hounds, hoping that the young dogs will get some serious on-the-job training. While it may seem that having more dogs on a chase is better, this is not necessarily the case. Too many dogs can result in confusion and chaos, lost dogs and wasted time. If the bear is bayed up on the ground and a fight ensues, too many dogs mean that one or two may get mauled simply because they get trapped by their packmates as they try to dodge the bear. Houndsmen have individual comfort zones when it comes to the number of hounds they like to run.

TRAINING & CONDITIONING

Good hunting hounds are already in shape when the hunters arrive. The houndsman will condition his dogs in several ways. He may tie them to a rope attached to a moving wheel, allowing them to run in the kennel area. He may take them for walks on a leash as he scouts the country. One excellent way to train hounds is during what many states call their "pursuit" season, a time when it is legal to run bears or cats with hounds but not kill them. This gives the dogs a chance to get into top physical shape and get back into the swing of chasing game.

Young dogs often learn to follow bears by first tracking a piece of old bear hide on a rope that a trainer drags along the ground to leave a scent trail. The trainer will walk a long distance with the drag, making several turns and twists in the trail to simulate the path a real bears takes. The trainer will lay the scent trail down while the dog cannot see it, then leave a head or hide hidden at the end. A pup that successfully finds the head or hide is rewarded.

FIELD TRANSPORT

There are as many ways to transport hounds to the field as there are houndsmen. Most hounds are transported in the bed of a pickup or flatbed truck in dog boxes designed for the purpose. The bottoms of the boxes are lined with hay for insulation and ease of cleaning.

Dog boxes serve many purposes. They protect each dog from the elements, and give each its own place to lie down and rest. They also keep

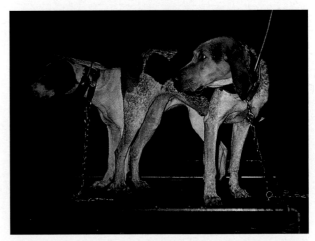

When cruising roads looking for a fresh track, many houndsmen keep strike dogs chained to the top of their boxes. Up there, the hounds can more easily smell fresh bear sign.

the dogs away from each other, which prevents fights and tangled lead ropes. The boxes must have adequate ventilation so that the dogs can cool down easily after a long, hard chase, yet not be so open to the air that they chill in cold late-fall and winter weather.

When searching for fresh bear tracks, hounds-men often slowly cruise backcountry roads in their trucks. One or two dogs might each be removed from its box and chained to the top of the box so the dog can ride comfortably, yet more easily smell any lingering bear scent. The first time I ever saw this trick I thought, "Yeah buddy, this guy doesn't have a clue!" The clueless one turned out to be me, as his hounds smelled a slug of bears from the back of the truck that week.

RADIO COLLARS

Virtually all professional houndsmen today attach radio collars on at least a few of their dogs. These collars serve many purposes. For one thing, they make it possible to keep track of the hounds as they chase bears over the big, deep, wide and often roadless canyons found in many Western wilderness areas, or across the vast forest-and-swamp regions found elsewhere in bear country. If the dogs lose the bear and then cannot find the truck again, the collar makes it easy to locate the dog. The collars also have nameplates attached, with the houndsman's name, address and phone number, so the dog can be returned if another person should find it.

There are some hunters who are against the use of radio collars on hounds, and that is fine. But most hunters use radio collars with the express purpose of using the signal only to find wayward dogs, and not to gain an electronic advantage over the bear. The collars provide a measure of protection for the houndsman against losing a valuable dog. They also help the dog's owner locate his hound should it be injured or killed, which happens on occasion.

LET'S GO HUNTING WITH HOUNDS ...

Okay, now that you have a basic understanding of what hounds are all about, it's time to go bear hunting behind a pack of trained dogs. Turn the page and let's get going.

Radio collars are standard equipment when hound hunting. These collars are used to help a houndsman relocate his dogs after they have taken off in pursuit of a bear over rugged country, not as an electronic advantage over the bears.

HUNTING WITH HOUNDS

I was absolutely exhausted. We had followed the hounds in the truck for a couple of hours, paralleling the deep, brush-choked Oregon canyon in which they were running the bear as we tried to keep track of what was happening and figure out where the chase would eventually end up. When guide Dave Handrich made that decision, we parked, jumped out and took off on foot.

That's when the rain began—a freezing, sleety mess following two days of wet snow that surprised us in late October. The ground and flora were saturated and as slippery as an oil slick. Of course we had to park the truck below where the dogs were running, so we started the trek with a

1,000-foot climb up the slope. Moving as fast as we could, we reached the elevation that we thought the dogs were at, and cut hard left. It was tough going, and took us more than two hours to finally reach the tree.

The hounds had certainly done their job. Up the tree was a dandy boar, the dogs yapping and barking around the trunk as they kept him in place. Handrich carefully looked the bear over and decided that this was, indeed, a darn nice one. As his son moved in to leash up the hounds, I readied my old, battered pre-1964 Model 70 Win. in .30-06. Most bear guides move their dogs away from the tree before a shot is taken, in case the

Well-conditioned hounds can cover many, many miles of tough country in pursuit of a black bear that can easily cover the same, or more, distance. If you book a hound hunt, the best advice anyone can give you: Get yourself in shape!

The purpose of running bears with hounds is to get the bear to run up a tree, where it will stay until the hunters arrive and can decide whether or not the bear is one they wish to harvest.

bear falls to the hounds and, still living, works the dogs over.

About that time, the old bruin decided that the tree was not the place to be. If you have never seen a big bear climb or descend a tree trunk, the speed at which they can do so will flat startle you. This was my first experience, and when I saw the bear start down the tree so fast, I was so shocked that I almost forgot the purpose of the exercise.

When Dave said something like, "If you want him, you better take him NOW!" I put a 165-grain Remington Core-Lokt bullet through his lungs. He tumbled out of the tree right into the middle of dog handler and dogs, and together they rolled down the slope out of sight in a tangled, barking mess.

Fortunately, the bear was dead.

When we finally sorted all that out, it was raining to beat the band. I took very few pictures, then Handrich gutted the bear and tied a short rope to his two front legs. As it began to rain even harder, we began dragging the carcass down that muddy slope. I am not sure which of us fell down more often, but I do remember it took an hour to get to the truck. We were all soaked to the bone, colder than an Alaska winter night and flat filthy. We drove back to camp and everyone immediately hit the sack. The next day, the sky didn't

clear, but it did stop pouring frozen water on our heads, making the skinning and butchering chores reasonably pleasant.

My first experience with hounds had yielded an old boar, with an estimated body weight of 350 pounds. The bear's flawless, luxurious hide squared 6 feet 3 inches. Like most uninitiated hound hunters, I had thought the hunt was going to be a piece of cake. How wrong I was.

LOCATING A BEAR TO RUN

The first thing you need to do on a hound hunt is locate a very fresh track or scent trail for the dogs to follow. Most houndsmen try to make sure that the track being followed is a large one, to keep from wasting time chasing small bears or sows with cubs.

In a few areas, the use of hounds is combined with baiting. Here the hunters set bear baits and, when they are hit, try to locate tracks to see if the bear is a large one. Then the hunters will bring the dogs in and turn them loose. Generally the

A hound hunt begins when a fresh track is located. An experienced guide can tell by the size and shape of the track whether a sow, young boar, or a mature boar—the kind you want to take—left the track.

In the Western mountains, houndsmen will cover a massive amount of country in their truck, dogs in the back, in search of a fresh bear track to turn the dogs loose on. Depending on conditions and terrain, horses or snowmobiles may also be used.

bait is checked in the evening and again in the morning. If it has been hit both times, you can be sure the track the dogs will take up is fresh enough to run.

In the West, houndsmen will cover a massive amount of country seeking a fresh bear to chase. They do this in pickup trucks, on horseback or sometimes on snow machines if an early fall or late spring snow has fallen, making roads impassable by truck. To keep the strike dogs from exhaustion, the dogs are often positioned in the open bed of the truck or on top of their dog box, where they can smell a bear as the vehicle is slowly driven along backcountry roads. If you have never been around hounds, you will be amazed at how well they can smell from the truck bed.

When the hound smells a bear it will bark loudly. The houndsman will then stop the truck and look for the bear track. This way, he can be very selective about the size of bear he runs. Dave Handrich passed by several small bears in the week we hunted together in Oregon, before turning the

hounds loose on the bear I eventually killed.

If there are more vehicles and hunters than strike dogs, some hunters may simply cruise the roads looking for tracks. When they find one that seems fresh and large enough to follow, they can contact the vehicle with the dogs by radio. If the roads are sandy and vehicular traffic is low, the hunters may "drag" the roads in the evening by pulling a log or similar object that will wipe out any old tracks, making it easier to spot a fresh track the following morning.

While the search for fresh tracks is concentrated in the morning, it is possible to find fresh tracks any time of day. However, if tracks are found too late in the day, it is likely you won't turn the dogs loose. There are few problems worse than having the dogs out chasing a bear after dark, while you're trying to find them.

THE CHASE

A chase can last anywhere from a few minutes—rare as a four-leaf clover—to several hours.

THERE HE IS!

The object is to get the bear up a tree, where the hunter can move into position for the shot in a controlled manner, without fear of the bear running off again or engaging the dogs in a fight. When the bear is properly treed, life is good, although as mentioned earlier, treed bears do not always like to stay treed, and you have to be ready for anything. There are times, though, when the bear will simply not tree, and the dogs have it bayed up on the ground. This usually happens in thick cover where visibility is limited to a few yards at most. The hunter must then approach quietly from downwind, attempting to get a shot without the bear knowing he is there.

If the bear is on the ground, you have to be very careful that you do not shoot a dog by mistake, either with a miss or a bullet that passes through the bear.

LET'S GO!

Not all chases result in a caught bear. Bears, and especially wise old boars that may have been run by hounds before, have plenty of evasive tricks. They may swim rivers, ponds or lakes to erase their scent. They may walk logs across deep chasms or rivers, or backtrack their own trails. They may simply refuse to tree or bay up, instead swatting at the hounds and continuing on, eventually running the day out before the hunters can catch up. Just because the hounds have been turned loose, there's no guarantee of success.

That's one of the things that make hound hunting so exciting and enjoyable.

The only sure thing is the fact that during the course of a week's hunt, something unexpected and unpredictable will happen. When success finally does come, it's always a true team effort. That, and the joy of watching a pack of trained hounds work and seeing how they bring a sense of pride and accomplishment to a true houndsman's face, are why I continue to follow the sound of the hounds.

(Note: Bear hunting with hounds is not legal in all states. See page 155 for game department resources where you can find out about your hunting region's current regulations.)

Not all chases result in caught bears. When you do arrive at the tree, however, and are rewarded with the mature boar up high and the hounds howling and barking below, it is a step back in time, to when man depended on his dogs to help him survive. It is a great feeling, indeed.

During the chase, the houndsman will strain to stay within hearing of his dogs. Once the bear has been treed or bayed up, the dogs will change the pitch of their barking. The houndsman can recognize this, and then steer you toward the spot where your bear will be found.

All sorts of things can happen during the chase. The dogs can run out of earshot. They can lose the bear entirely. The bear may double back over the road, when the houndsman may turn a couple of fresh dogs out on him. Generally speaking, as a client, it is your job to stay out of the houndsman's way and to keep up. So get in shape! (See page 97 for suggestions.)

Hunting Black Bears

Get in Shape for Hound Hunting

While it may at first appear that hunting bears with dogs is a piece of cake, in truth, you need to be in good physical condition to follow hounds hot on a bear's track. You'll probably be led through some nasty, rough country, and the chase can take many hours. You have to be able to keep up, and that means being in good aerobic condition.

Aerobic literally means "with oxygen." You need to train to improve your aerobic capacity, strengthening your legs, lungs and heart. That means aerobic exercise.

The first step is to visit your doctor for a checkup. Once he clears you to begin your program, there are several ways to get started. The easiest is to visit a local health club, gym or YMCA and enroll in some sort of aerobics class. There are several that will help you build a strong aerobic base. Aerobic dance and step classes are excellent. Jogging, bicycling and swimming are superb. Jumping rope is hard to beat.

A benefit of beginning at a health club or gym is that you can take advantage of the services of a trained fitness professional. They can explain to you how to determine your maximum heart rate and, from that, your training heart rate, the rate you want to achieve and maintain during exercise. These professionals can also help you monitor your progress and set up a program designed to meet your fitness goal.

Your goal is to be able to hike quickly through rough country, possibly mountains, without slowing down and falling too far behind the chase. To achieve this, you need to employ specificity training, a term athletes use to describe training for a specific event. For example, sprinters don't lift a lot of weights with their upper bodies, instead concentrating on training their legs, lungs and heart, primarily by running or bicycling. You should do the same.

The best exercise of all for this type of active hunting is to carry a weighted daypack while quickly walking in hilly country. If no steep hills are close by, walk quickly up and down stadium steps or the stairs at work. In the gym, do leg exercises with weights. This will give you the strength to hike, climb and get through thick brush. Coupled with exercises that increase aerobic capacity, like jogging, swimming, bicycling and so on, you'll build a base of aerobic fitness and strength in the specific muscle groups you'll use most when bear hunting.

While not as important as aerobic conditioning and specificity training, employing a program of weight training will supplement your conditioning and make you all the tougher once you're in bear country.

Following hounds can be one of the most physically demanding activities you'll ever experience. A smart hunter will get in shape to meet the challenge.

x

Chapter 6

OTHER BEAR-BUSTING TECHNIQUES

Pennsylvania biologist Gary Alt is one of the country's foremost experts on black bears. Years ago he told me something that still sticks with me to this day. "Most bear hunters here in the East go into the woods, sit on a stump and hope a bear comes by," Alt said. "Unless they are awfully lucky, these hunters have very little chance of killing a bear."

In big game hunting, there is more than one way to get a black bear. There are the more traditional methods that have worked well for eons: spot-and-stalk hunting, baiting and hound hunting. Then there are those off-the-wall techniques that just seem to do a better job in certain places under certain circumstances.

Hunters working the coastal region of British Columbia and Alaska hunt from the salt water in boats. Here the weather can be horrible, the crashing surf and jagged rocks a nightmare, and the aggressive bears quite dangerous. A guide must be both an expert seaman and a superb bear guide. It's an example of a different type of hunting adapted to unique local conditions.

Have you ever tried calling bears? It works, and at times the bears come to a predator-type call as aggressively as a bull to a red cape. It is not for the faint of heart.

How about driving thick swampland, twisted hollows or other patches of thick cover, trying to push bears past standers à la deer hunting? Or slipping along a creek, hoping to catch a bear feeding in a small meadow? Or setting a treestand along a beech ridge when the nuts are dropping? Or watching an apple orchard or cornfield where the sign of feeding bears is strong?

When hunting black bears, you have to be able to adapt to the conditions at hand. Here's how …

BEARS BY BOAT

The client was a hotshot treestand whitetail hunter from the East Coast, a guy who thought he was tough and cool and ready to play with the big boys. He'd taken a handful of good bucks from an exclusive parcel of private land his money allowed him to hunt, but he'd never stalked big game from the ground. He was about to get educated.

The first bear he missed was a gimme. Guide James Boyce dropped the two of us off on a large jumble of kelp-covered boulders among the pounding surf, which muffled the skiff noise. The bear was calmly feeding at 18 yards when the arrow passed under his belly. Fortunately, the big bruin turned and ran back into the thick old-growth forest. The next time, Hotshot wasn't so lucky.

This was a bruiser bear, a monster that fed out onto an open beach late one afternoon. Boyce, another guide named Duncan MacPhail and the two hunters (Hotshot and his father) skiffed ashore as I watched from our anchored boat/camp, Gunsmoke. The four stalked to within 40 yards, when Hotshot decided that he'd be the

Hunting monster black bears along the coast of Southeast Alaska and coastal British Columbia is one of the most exciting big game hunting adventures in North America.

On coastal hunts, hunters cruise the coastline in small boats and glass for bears that emerge from the old-growth forest to feed at beaches and small, rocky points. Once a bear is spotted, you beach the boat and stalk him on foot.

one to take the bear. As Duncan ran my video camera, Hotshot stalked to within 20 yards of the feeding bruin, drew and released. The arrow flew right over the bear's back, clattering among the rocks.

Instead of running back into the trees, this alpha bear decided he'd eliminate the competition. In a flash, he wheeled and charged the hunter, who for some reason had decided to stalk the bear in the wide open, and not use the many available large boulders and logs for cover.

Fortunately, Boyce had instructed Hotshot's father to immediately shoot the bear if his son muffed his chance. Dad was a crack shot, getting off three quick rounds from his .270 and saving his son from a serious swatting. That bear, a beautiful coal-black boar, squared more than 7 feet, with a skull measuring more than 20 inches. He weighed nearly 500 pounds.

Hotshot couldn't believe he had missed. In fact, he threw a temper tantrum that would have made a five-year-old proud, insisting there was no way he could have muffed such a slam-dunk shot. But he did. Big black bears have a way of doing that to you.

If you think black bear hunting is boring, noth-ing more than sitting up a tree waiting for a bear to come to a bait, you haven't hunted bears by boat in southeast Alaska or along the British Columbia coast. Like the country in which they live, the bears are big and tough and unforgiving, the dominant predator in an environment that can turn on you in a heartbeat. Likewise, the bears can turn on you in a heartbeat. Hunting these bears is a real old-fashioned adventure.

SOUTHEAST ALASKA: BEAR HEAVEN

Alaska is a great enigma. Visitors will tell you it's the driest, wettest, hottest, coldest, snowiest, dustiest place they've ever seen—sometimes all in the same day. During a spring week in southeast Alaska, you can reasonably expect days that are so bright it hurts your eyes, and others so dark you're not sure whether your watch says it's lunch time or midnight. And as one old-timer once said, where else but the windward slopes of the south-east Alaska coastline can it rain so much that when a wolf raises his head to howl, he drowns before he can get his mouth shut?

When spring rolls around and the days begin to lengthen, you forget all that. As the winter

Alaska's coastal panhandle and adjacent islands are where the state's best black bear hunting—and largest bears—are located.

mainland and islands are comprised of virgin forest, still untouched by the hand of man. In some places, logging roads cut through the country, and there you can hunt from a vehicle. For the most part, though, a boat is used to cover the area.

Both residents and nonresidents are allowed to hunt black bears unguided in Alaska. Safely hunting them by boat, however, requires more than the necessary hunting skills and equipment. To safely navigate the often treacherous waters of southeast Alaska, you must have not only an extremely high level of seamanship skills, but also well-maintained equipment designed specifically for the job and the experience to know when—and when not—to challenge the weather. In Alaska, those who choose to confront nature can wind up in a bad way. Or dead.

James Boyce of Baranof Expeditions (P.O. Box 3107, Sitka, AK 99835; 907/747-3934) is the kind of man you want to hunt this country with. An ex-Navy Special Forces man, Jim has lived and guided out of Sitka for more than a decade. His equipment is first-class. His skills both in handling

snow recedes off the beaches and up the timbered slopes, you know the region's black bears will soon emerge from their dens, ravenous with hunger and sporting the thickest, most luxurious coats of the year. It's definitely time to go bear hunting!

The panhandle of southeast Alaska is famous for its high bear densities, of both the black and grizzly (or brown) bear varieties. The region consists of a thin strip of mainland mountain country and numerous islands, all of which are covered in thick old-growth timber and sliced by rivers and streams that tumble and fall as they make their way from the glacier country to the sea. The mountain faces are tangled with berry bushes and other lush forbs that bears love, while the beaches feature large sections of washed-up kelp and grassy tidal estuaries that draw ravenous spring bears like a magnet. The state's small game and deer populations also feed both black and brown bears to some extent, especially in late fall and early winter when the region's massive salmon runs have petered out. If you were to ask for an ideal habitat to be created for bears to thrive and grow large, you wouldn't get better than southeast Alaska.

HUNTING BY BOAT

With few exceptions, there are no roads in much of southeast Alaska. The majority of the

One reason to hunt coastal Alaska and British Columbia is the preponderance of mature boars. A hunter who hunts hard and passes up smaller bears has an excellent chance at success on the biggest bear of his life.

Hunting Black Bears

his custom-made 36-foot aluminum-hulled big boat, Gunsmoke, and in running his 17-foot skiff through the often wildly pounding surf and always-dangerous rocks to load and unload hunters, is first-rate. That he thinks like a bear is a bonus.

The hunting goes like this. At times, you spot bears feeding along the beaches from the larger boat as you move "camp" to a fresh area. Most of the time, though, you patrol the beaches in an open skiff, glassing for bears that have stepped out of the thick old-growth timber to feed among the huge jumbles of logs and large piles of beached kelp. You might also beach the skiff and hike inland to glass large, grassy estuaries for bears feeding on the succulent new grasses of spring.

Early in the season, you see fewer bears than later on, as most bears are either still in their dens or just emerging from high-country denning areas and not yet down to the beaches. Generally speaking, though, these "early" bears are more likely to be large boars, as they are the first to come out of the dens. These are prime-time trophy bears with long, luxurious, unrubbed pelts.

Later in the season, from late April through late

Small skiffs must be able to handle rough water, putt into tight covers or work along an open shoreline. Seamanship skills are essential for handling these boats safely in rough water and bad weather.

May, it isn't unusual to spot between 20 and 40 bears a day on the beaches, though many are sows with cubs at that time.

Once a bear is spotted, you get close enough by boat to look him over thoroughly before committing to a stalk. If he's big enough and his hide is unrubbed, it's time to secure the big boat, jump in

When bears emerge from the forest to the beaches, they can sometimes be seen traveling as they search for food. When you're making the stalk, keep the wind in your face at all times.

a skiff, and make your move. The skiff is securely beached downwind of the bear, and the stalk begins.

Because of the location of the beaches—the bears seem to prefer relatively small pocket-type beaches over broader, more open ones—you can usually stalk to within 100 yards relatively easily. The winds are always blowing to keep your scent from a bear's radar nose, and the sound of the crashing surf covers any inadvertent noises you might make. Getting a controlled, close-range shot is pretty routine.

During a recent spring, Boyce, assistant guide Eric Johnson and I were cruising the beaches in search of a good bear. After looking over 14 other bears, we spotted "him" late one afternoon as he fed on a small beach. We skiffed ashore and stalked to within 40 yards. Eric ran the video as I moved another 20 yards closer, waited for the bear to turn quartering away and turned my Mathews Q2 loose. The Beman carbon shaft buried to the fletching, and the bear didn't go 20 yards before piling up. His hide squared 7 feet 6 inches and his skull measured more than 20 inches. Black bears just don't get any better than this.

SEE YOU THERE!

One year, I brought four good friends on a hunt with Boyce and another top guide, Scott Newman. All took giant bears in an incredible week of bear hunting, but one typical of spring hunting in southeast Alaska. The days were sunny and warm, overcast and rainy. We saw a lot of bears, and had the kind of adventurous skiff-riding and stalking that the gang will be telling their grandchildren about.

The last evening, two days of constant rain had finally stopped. As we returned to the big boat at dark that last night, the stars overpowered the deep black of the night sky. And then, as if on cue, the northern lights danced for us as only they can do, lighting up both the night and our hearts. Where else but in Alaska can sportsmen still find such untouched wilderness filled with such an abundance of wildlife and beauty?

You can be sure I'll be going back, again and again.

This is what it is all about: Guide James Boyce, left, client Glenn Crowther, and a giant black bear (arrow) walking right at them, not 30 feet from where they are set up. Does it get any more exciting than this?

BUCK WAYS FOR BLACK BEARS

In many parts of the country, most black bears are taken incidentally when hunting deer or elk. Systematically taking a bear requires careful planning and knowledge of bear habits and haunts.

Black bear hunting is not easy. These secretive, often nocturnal animals live their lives in relative obscurity, staying to thick cover and avoiding people whenever they can. Even in areas where bear populations are relatively high, there still are not many of them when compared to more common big game species like deer and elk. Also, with a few exceptions—like bears concentrating on salmon streams in summer and early fall—most of the time, black bears are widely scattered throughout their available range.

In fact, Gary Alt, the well-known Pennsylvania Game Commission biologist who headed that state's bear program for many years, once told me that by far the highest percentage of bear kills in his state were the result of nothing more than pure luck. "Most bear hunters here in the East go into the woods, sit on a stump and hope a bear comes by," Alt said. "Unless they are awfully lucky, these hunters have very little chance of killing a bear." Alt said that a survey conducted among Pennsylvania hunters showed that 13 percent of successful bear hunters shot the first bear they had ever seen in the wild, and 53 percent had seen fewer than six wild bears total in their lifetimes—and this included all hunting trips as well as trips to such bear-rich environments as Yellowstone Park.

Using hounds or baits can increase your chances of success on black bears, but the truth is that in most states, one or both of these methods has been banned. That means that to be successful on a black bear hunt, you're going to have to treat it just like you would a serious hunt for a big buck deer.

KEY ON PREFERRED FOOD SOURCES

Regardless of where you hunt bears, always remember one thing—a black bear is a large, furry food processor whose movements and habits are largely dictated by a seemingly insatiable appetite.

More than any other big game animal I've ever hunted, black bears tend to concentrate on specific food sources at specific times. Generally speaking, their preferred fall food sources are berries, mast crops and fruits, though in areas like Alaska and coastal British Columbia you can add migrating salmon to the list. In some states, agricultural crops, like corn, draw bears. In spring, bears love the first lush grasses that grow along water courses, on the steep sides of mountains and in swamps.

Your first step is to call a state game biologist and ask about the preferred foods in the area where you plan to hunt. In many mountainous Western states huckleberries, blueberries and blackberries draw bears in the fall. In California and Oregon, I've watched bears tear up manzanita patches and almost knock down laurel trees to get their berries. In the Southwest, black bears can eat every acorn dropped for miles and routinely flatten large patches of prickly pear cactus. In the East, acorn crops are a key food source, beechnuts can draw them like a magnet, and chokecherries, hazelnuts and black cherries are also good bear foods. Fruit orchards, especially apples, can also draw them like flies to honey. Skunk cabbage is bear candy wherever it's found. In the upper Midwest, blueberries are a draw, as are corn- and other cropfields cut into the wilderness.

You must remember, though, that bears do not act like deer. That is, when one specific food source has been depleted, they'll move on until they locate another. While deer may use an acorn ridge for a month, bears may be on it a week or less before leaving. Also, bears are very mobile animals. Alt's research has shown that some males will use an area of as much as 60 square miles,

Black bears love their "salad," believe it or not. Green, leafy, succulent food—leaves, stems, roots—are always high on a hungry bear's "preferred" list.

females 15 square miles, as a home range. They move all the while, looking for food.

Scouting Is Critical

Hunters who think they can take a black bear without scouting should stop off at the convenience store on the way home and buy a lottery ticket. That's the kind of luck it would take.

In addition to food sources, scout for scat, tracks, feeding activity like overturned rocks, dug-up anthills, decaying logs that have been torn up and places where bears have literally ripped branches from trees to get at the nuts. To get a handle on where bear activity is high, you must log a lot of scouting hours in the woods.

Also, ask lots of questions of locals, including whether there have been any recent bear sightings or any general areas where bears are seen from year to year. The locals may not be able to tell you exactly where the bears are living, but if you can find out information such as where the bears have been seen crossing a certain road lately, you now have a great place to begin scouting. Such information is only good immediately, though, as bears tend to move a lot. Sightings that occurred a month ago are rarely valuable.

In fall, berries are a key food source for black bears. Find large berry patches in bear country, and chances are good that a bruin or two will be nearby.

One indicator that there are bears in the area—and where to hunt for them—is checking bear scat for undigested food. This scat is filled with chokecherries; where do you think we should hunt?

One mistake novice bear hunters make is assuming the amount of time and effort they will need to put into a successful bear hunt is comparable to or less than that which they put into a white-tailed deer hunt. Nothing could be further from the truth. Deer are much more habitual and predictable than bears, and their overall numbers and densities are greater, making patterning deer movement easier.

Bears are very unpredictable in their movement patterns, but again, these movements are generally tied to the availability of food. And you can be sure that in years when preferred foods are scarce, bears will move more. If acorns are scarce one year but beechnuts are abundant, it makes sense to hunt beech ridges, not oak flats.

You can also scout in summer. In the Southwest, I often scout deer and bears at the same time. I glass during early morning and late evenings for deer, then during mid-day check out oak groves and cactus patches. If I find trees that bears had torn limbs off of the previous fall, I am reasonably sure that when these same trees produce next fall's nut crop, there will be a bear vacuuming them up.

In season, bear scat is an obvious sign. Bears living in a particular area often use the same general area to defecate daily. In the West, for example, it isn't unusual to find that bears use flat, open logging roads as a makeshift restroom. Find several piles of bear scat on a logging road, climb high and glass nearby ridges for berries, and the chances are good you'll spot a bear.

Other obvious sign includes rootings, torn-up anthills and old logs and climbing marks on nut trees into which bears have scampered to strip off the nuts. I also often walk along water courses and check out the largest evergreen trees for signs of claw marks, indicating that bears—usually sows with cubs—have climbed them during their travels.

Topographic maps can be a big help. Coupled with information from local residents and knowledge of what the bears prefer to eat in the area, topo maps can show you drainages leading to the food sources, and thickets that bears prefer to use for bedding areas. Or you can locate broken areas of thick cover between feeding and resting areas during daylight. Positioning yourself where you can see these areas without allowing bears to see you makes good sense.

Topographic maps can be a big help when hunting black bears. Maps can show you the drainages leading to preferred food sources identified by biologists and local experts, and the thickets bears prefer for daytime bedding areas.

A black bear is really little more than a giant food processor, always searching for its next meal. Knowing what they prefer to eat at any given time, and where it is located, is the key to hunting bears the "buck way."

HUNTING BEARS THE BUCK WAY

Bears move primarily at night, though when they're not heavily pressured you can catch them out during the day. I've found that late evening is by far the best time to take a bear. Bears like to move just before dark, feed at night, then retreat to the nastiest, thickest place around to bed for the day. Swamps, cool timbered ridges, overgrown clear cuts and the like, are the kinds of places bears like to bed. Stationing yourself between the bedding area and the food source is a great way to get a shot at a black bear.

In the intermountain West, I find it best to pick a spot where I can see a lot of country, and glass. If there's food around—berries, nuts and so on—and it's a good bear area, sooner or later you'll spot a bear. Look mostly along the edges of timber stringers, thick brush and the edges between nasty cover and more open feeding areas. In the thicker country of the East and Midwest, scouting and finding sign, then hunting the area more like you would for deer, is the best way to spot bears.

In areas where bears like to feed on agricultural crops, it can be very productive to scout field edges for bear sign, then set a treestand in the hopes of intercepting the bruin as he comes to

raid the standing corn or rip the fruit off the apple trees. If the bears are not reaching the fields until after shooting hours are over, hunt them like you would a deer—that is, backtrack their trails and set stands in the woods, off the field edges 100 to 150 yards. Hunting the edges of large crop fields is one time when the hunter will want to carry a rifle that enables him to make a shot out to 250 yards or so.

When hunting bears, remember that they are secretive creatures with a tremendous sense of smell.

Always remember that a bear has a superb sense of smell and can see better than you think. When setting up a spotting station, planning a still-hunt or setting a treestand or ground blind, always keep the wind in your favor. When on stand, don't unnecessarily skyline yourself or

Station yourself between a bear bedding area and food source to intercept a traveling bruin.

move around more than you have to. When I get on a glassing or spotting station, I get myself nice and comfy, then remain still except to raise and lower my binoculars for a look. And when looking for bears, remember that they spend as little time in the open as they can. Focus your efforts on thick cover, especially the upper edges of the thick stuff where bears can walk easily yet dive into their security cover in a flash.

Beating the Bush for Bears

A great way to hunt black bears is with groups of hunters who conduct drives through prime bear habitat. This is especially effective in swamps and bogs—areas that are very tough to hunt by stalking or spotting.

Bear drives should be conducted just like drives for deer. That is, hunters should be in a known bear area. The drive master should be familiar with the topography and have some knowledge of the locale's bear movement patterns. Standers are placed either in treestands or on clumps of ground that offer good visibility, where they wait for the drivers—who also carry firearms, as their chances of getting the shot are almost as good as that of the standers—as the drivers work their way through the thick cover, hoping to move a bear into a stander's sights. Great care must be taken not to take shots at sows with cubs.

Driving can be a great way for a group to get a shot at a bear. "In Pennsylvania, hunters who know what they are doing on drives predictably kill bears every year," said Gary Alt. "It doesn't really matter which person shoots the bear, it is a group effort and all share in the spoils."

In many areas—including those dominated by swamps and bogs—conducting drives through prime bear habitat is a good way to get a shot. Drives should be conducted as they are for deer, with a "drive master" who's intimate with the terrain and who has some knowledge of the bears' local movement patterns.

CALLING ALL BEARS

*J*im and I were set up on a bald knob overlooking a large patch of Arizona's semi-desert foothill country. I had never thought of such an area as being a good place for black bears, but in truth this region holds some of the country's biggest bears. Below was a vast expanse of sagebrush and prickly pear cactus, flat ground interspersed with rolling hills and deep cuts. Jim assured me that there were several good bears here.

Bears are always hungry, and a screaming rabbit promises an easy, protein-filled meal.

We glassed for a while and didn't see anything, so Jim began using his dying rabbit predator call. It was just like calling coyotes. We were camouflaged and ready to rumble.

Before long, a very large black bear showed himself. I couldn't believe it! He made a beeline toward our station, sniffing the air and leaving no doubt as to what was on his mind—supper. And we were on the menu.

The closer the bear got, the more his hackles stood at attention. This guy was ready to rumble too. When he went out of sight at the base of our hill, Jim stopped calling and picked up his .30-06. I had my bow, and was starting to get worried. It was deathly quiet when, all of a sudden, the bear popped up not 20 yards away, heading right for Jim. I drew my bow and shot the bear through the chest. This diverted his attention from my buddy, who had his rifle up and the safety off. The bear whirled and ran down the hill, where he died.

Both Jim and I were shaking like leaves. "Holy mackerel, Batman!" I said. (Or something like that.) "This bear calling can be scary!" My friend just shook his head and grinned. "Yeah," he said. "When they come to the predator call, they are not making a social visit. They are ready to eat the caller!"

CALLING BEARS

Yes, black bears can be called. And it can be more than a little exciting. In fact, it can be downright dangerous, if you're not buttoned up. I learned right away that you never call bears alone, but only hunt with a buddy who can watch your back.

Black bears are omnivores. They eat anything, including lots of meat whenever they can catch it or find a carcass. In areas where there are lots of rabbits, they will come to the dying rabbit call as readily as any predator will. They'll also come to a fawn distress call, as I later learned while hunting black bears in Alaska.

Like all game, bears will not come to the call every time they hear it. I have also found more success by first spotting a bear at a long distance, then calling it to me, as opposed to calling blind. The exception is if I know there is a bear in the area, in which case I may try some blind calling.

I have also noticed that bears lose interest in the call quickly. By that I mean that as long as you are calling they will come to you. Stop blowing the call, however, and they are as apt to sit down as keep coming. Steady calling is important.

You can call bears up with odd things too. One

Black bears will, at times, come to skillfully crafted predator calls. But be ready; when a bear comes, he is ready to eat the caller!

time I was sitting in a treestand in the Finger Lakes region of New York State, bowhunting whitetails. I tried some rattling, and when I heard a branch break I got pumped up. It was not a big buck, however, but a big black bear. He walked past at 20 yards, went down the deer trail and stopped. I used the grunt call, and his ears perked up. Then he vanished, and I thought it was all over. Next thing I knew, he was right under my tree, looking up at me! Fortunately I was able to shoo him off. Now when I call black bears, I always have a "hammer" with me—a large-caliber handgun, rifle or fully charged can of pepper spray.

MORE INFORMATION

Before you call bears, you need more information than can be provided here so you can understand exactly what's involved. One great source is a chapter of the NAHC's book *Hunting Predators— Proven Tactics That Work* by Gordy Krahn. This book is available from the club by calling 1-800-922-4868 (item code HLNHP).

Chapter 7

TRACKING WOUNDED BEARS

Even in the glare of the lantern, the blood trail was faint. It was dark and the trail ran into an endless sea of alders. It was a tangled jungle, and the thought of tracking several hundred pounds of poorly hit black bear had the hackles on the back of my neck standing at attention.

The two of us moved forward slowly, one using the lantern to follow the blood trail and paw prints, the other shining the powerful flashlight ahead searching for the glow of eyes, each of us clutching our big rifles firmly. We took the track around a small knob, down into a hollow and across a small creek. After 300 yards, we stopped to regroup.

That's when we heard it—a low guttural growling that had us both jumping out of our boots. Fortunately, the bear was not able to do anything more than growl. When we found him 50 yards farther, he had already died. My heart didn't stop jumping for hours.

While most bears are recovered quickly without incident, tracking a wounded black bear can be bad news. The cover is always thick, the blood trail usually skimpy, and night often has fallen, or nearly so. Because every bear has the potential to cause you big trouble, every bear you trail should be followed up with the assumption that it is still alive and ready to bite you. Better to be safe than sorry. You need the right tools, some basic tracking skills and a heightened sense of alertness to get the job done.

If you hunt bears, you need to know how to find them after the shot. Here's how to recover your bear efficiently and safely.

Although you should not be fearful when trailing a black bear you've shot, you should nevertheless respect him. He is a big, powerful and wild survivor. The best tracking job starts with a well-placed and lethal shot.

Hunting Black Bears

How to Follow the Tracks Safely

*I*t was near dark when the big boar came to the bait. I knew he was the one I wanted, so when he presented a slight quartering-away angle as he dug into the ground bait I had prepared, I let my arrow fly. The hit appeared good, though you can never be sure at twilight. The boar grunted, spun rapidly around and crashed off into the incredibly thick jungle. Then, all was quiet.

I sat and calmed my nerves for a moment and replayed the shot in my mind. It felt good, and I was as sure as I could be that the bear was down not far from the bait site.

And yet ... I wasn't completely sure. So after 30 minutes, I quietly climbed down, hiked to the truck and drove into town to get my friend Lee. He quickly got dressed and grabbed his .338 Win. Mag. I had my lever-action .358 Win. with me, and we were off.

We approached the bait quietly and cautiously, then found my arrow. It had dark, bubbly blood, the sign of a lung hit. I showed Lee where the bear had disappeared into the brush and we spread out, 30 yards apart, our powerful headlamps shining brightly. Lee took the blood trail and I moved slightly above him, covering his flank. Thankfully, our caution this night was unfounded. The big bear was piled up 50 steps from the bait.

I made this recovery the way I did for two reasons. One, a wounded black bear can be a dangerous animal, especially in the thick brush after dark. Also, I had once been by myself when I followed up a bear that a friend had shot. The bear was poorly hit, and I ended up walking up on a bear with a fair amount of life left in him. I was on my hands and knees crawling through a horrible brushy tan-gle, but fortunately, I had my rifle in front of me and was able to get the finishing shot off before he got to me.

The key in following up any black bear is to use caution. We think of black bears more like Yogi than the Tasmanian Devil, but believe me, these big, strong, powerful animals can literally knock your block off.

Look & Listen

The tracking job begins with good shot placement. A black bear hit through both lungs with a pencil eraser is not going to go far. A bear hit too far back with a .375 H&H Mag. can go forever. Take your time to make that first shot count, and the tracking job will be short and sweet.

After the shot, watch the bear closely. See how he reacts to the hit, how he looks when he runs off, and mark the last spot you can physically see him enter the thick stuff. Also, be quiet and listen.

Most of the time a black bear is shot in thick cover, often near dark. That can make tracking him both difficult and, at times, dangerous. Always use extreme caution.

Listen for the sound of the bear running through the woods. If he runs beyond hearing distance, you'll have to undertake a possibly long and tedious tracking job. If the bear is hit well, the odds are good he will go no more than 75 to 100 yards, and you will hear him go down.

Also, bears shot through the lungs often emit what the African professional hunters call a "death bellow," a low moaning sound that you'll never forget once you hear it. If you hear this moaning, you can be reasonably sure your bear is down for the count. Pick a tree or other prominent landmark in line with this sound so you have a good idea where the bear may be located.

Still, the prudent hunter will follow the bear cautiously, always on the alert for trouble. In the world of bear tracking, it is better to be needlessly prepared than to be careless and surprised by several hundred pounds of hurt, angry fangs and claws.

THE BLOOD TRAIL

Even well-hit black bears are notorious for leaving a poor blood trail. Their thick muscles, fatty underlayer and luxurious hair impede blood from

Fluorescent ribbon is most helpful to mark a blood trail when following up a bear in the nasty thickets to which they invariably run after being shot.

freely dripping to the ground. That means a painstaking tracking job.

One time in southeast Alaska, I watched a bowhunter shoot a nice boar low through the right front leg. We tracked that bear for more than a mile, picking up a spot of blood here, a speck of blood there, and never did recover him. This is common. Bears shot through the large leg muscles with no broken bones are not fatally hit and are rarely recovered by hunters.

Even bears hit perfectly may not bleed much externally. I have followed many skimpy blood trails to a dead bear. During these tracking jobs, I also look for other sign, such as tracks, broken brush, and blood specks on waist-high brush and tree trunks. I also use the lay of the land to try to anticipate the bear's line of travel. Contrary to popular belief, I have seen many mortally wounded black bears initially race off uphill. They tend to want to leave the area along the same path from which they came. Always mark the trail with fluorescent flagging tape.

If you cannot find the bear or you lose the blood trail, backtrack and try circling the area slowly, always on the alert for another speck of blood or the bear itself.

Black bears are notorious for leaving a skimpy blood trail. Take your time and look for other sign—like tracks—as well as drops of blood.

TRACKING DOGS

When available, a good bear dog is the best insurance for recovering your bear. Nothing on earth can find your bear faster or more efficiently than a good hound's nose. If you have hounds, or know someone who does, and you are having trouble locating your bear, don't be afraid to bring the dogs into play. They can even find downed bears several hours after the fact.

Although most tracking jobs will be routine, any bear-trailing should be viewed as a potential problem. There is always that one-in-a-thousand chance that something can go wrong. Failure to use caution and all the tools at your disposal—including help from friends—is simply foolish.

A tracking dog skilled in following a blood trail is the best insurance against losing a bear's blood trail.

Tools of the Trade

There are several items that will make tracking bears in thick cover easier and safer. Here are a few suggestions.

Headlamp, lanterns. Tracking bears in the dark necessitates the best light you can use. Headlamps, like those from Petzl, and like that of the Mighty Max Camo Lite, which has a rechargeable 6-volt battery pack, keep your hands free and emit lots of light. Coleman lanterns are excellent as well, as are handheld lights like the Nite Tracker Rechargeable Spotlight, which puts out 2 million candlepower and has a rechargeable battery. Trust me, you can't have too much candlepower for this job.

Infra-red game finder. The Game Finder is a compact unit that picks up body heat and shows you the warmest place in the woods—and that's usually your bear. It takes some practice to use properly, but I have had success using one on black bears in thick forest cover.

Enhanced hearing. You can sharpen your hearing with a Walker's Game Ear I & II, a hearing enhancement device that fits easily into your ear and acts as a sort of hearing aid. It works very well.

Fluorescent flagging. The same stuff you use to mark blood trails in all big game hunting. It's invaluable.

A powerful light will make blood trailing after dark much easier. This is no time or place for small penlights!

Large-caliber firearm. Because it is usually legal to hunt bears with either a firearm or archery equipment, even when I'm bowhunting I like to have a firearm with me, just in case. Once the shot has been made, the bow stays behind and my rifle comes into play for the tracking job. A 12 gauge shotgun with slugs, or a rifle in .30-06 or larger, is my choice.

Chapter 8

TROPHY BLACK BEARS

*I*t happens to all of us on our first bear hunt. "There he is," you think as the first bear you've ever seen comes into view. "What a monster!" And then the doubts begin to creep in. Is he really a big one? Is it a boar or a sow? Geez, I'm not sure. How can I tell?

Judging black bears is not like field-judging deer or elk, which we've seen a million times either in person or in pictures. We know what a mature buck or bull looks like, and telling the difference between a male and female is easy.

Bears have no antlers or easily seen sex organs. Most hunters have no experience looking at bears. There are no familiar reference points. If there are two bears together, it is usually a sow and cub, and you're not hunting them. Boars generally travel alone, so you can't compare them side by side.

Learning to field-judge bears is particularly important if you hunt on your own. Experienced guides can help you judge them, of course, but even so, a rudimentary knowledge of the process will help you make the final decision when the guide says, "He's a pretty good one. Do you want him?" Believe me, nothing is more disappointing than taking a bear, then walking up and seeing him shrink right before your eyes.

Do you know how to tell a boar from a sow? Do you know how to field-judge black bears, both for size and the condition of the hide? How to square a bear hide? Measure a skull for the record book? The following pages will show you how to make sure that when the time comes to make a decision about whether this is the bear you want to take home with you, you can make the right choice.

Let's investigate …

WHAT IS A TROPHY BEAR?

*I*n all big game hunting, a trophy animal is in the eye of the beholder. That is, if it pleases you, you are satisfied with it and it is a trophy in your eyes, then it is indeed a trophy animal, regardless of size. In this case, though, when we are talking about trophy black bears, we are talking about the crème de la crème—the very best of the best.

When judging black bears for trophy quality, there are two things to look for: the size of the head and the quality of the hide.

SKULL SIZE

Because they have no obvious features, like antlers, that can be easily measured, bears are scored for record book purposes like cats—by the size of their skull.

Both the Boone & Crockett Club and the Pope & Young Club score skulls the same. First, all the flesh must be removed and the skull left to dry for 60 days before it can be officially measured. Then both the width of the skull and length of the lower jaw are measured. The numbers are added together and the total is the bear's official score, recorded in $1/16$-inch increments. (In Chapter 9, Meat & Trophy Care, we'll talk more about how to clean up a skull to maximize its score.)

The problem with hunting a bear "for the book" is that it is virtually impossible to tell by looking whether a bear's skull is large enough. There are a ton of variables that can affect how

A trophy black bear is a big, powerful, mature boar, an animal that dominates his world. A bear is entered into the record books based on the size of its skull.

B

A

$$\text{Bear Hide Square} = \frac{A + B}{2}$$

A bear hide is "squared" by first skinning the bear and removing the skull and paws, then laying the hide flat. Measure from tip of nose to tip of tail (A), and measure the distance between the two front paws (B). Add the numbers together and divide by two; the resulting number is the hide's "square."

large a skull appears, including how much muscle and fat the bear has on its head and jaws, as well as the thickness of the hide and the lushness of the hair. Skull size is a product of genetics, age and diet. Some bears may have lived a long life and have overly large bodies thanks to a great diet, but their skulls will never be of record-book size.

If you are hoping to take a record bear, your best chance is to hunt an area that has traditionally produced bears with skulls large enough to be included in one of the record books, then hunt hard until you find a large boar. After that, it's a crapshoot. I've taken bears I swore would have skulls big enough to make the book, only to find they come up short. But that's okay with me—I hunt them for their meat, body size and hides.

HIDE QUALITY

Perhaps the best measure of what makes a true "trophy" bear is the size and condition of the

hide. I know several very experienced bear guides, and all say the same thing: If the hide is large and the hair is lush, and the bear is a large-bodied and/or an old boar for the area, then the bear is a true trophy regardless of the size of the skull. If you ever go on a guided black bear hunt where the guide is with you when you are spotting bears (on many bait hunts you'll sit the bait alone), this is how he will judge the bear for you.

The size of a bear hide is commonly described by stating how big the hide "squared." To square a bear hide, you skin the bear out completely, and remove the skull and paws. Then lay the hide out on a flat surface, spreading the legs as wide as they can be spread in a natural position. Using a tape measure, measure the bear from the tip of its nose to the tip of its tail. Then measure across the chest and down the front legs, using the widest point from claw tip to claw tip. Add these two numbers together and divide them by two. The resulting number is the bear's "square" size.

Do not stretch the hide! This is a common trick some unscrupulous guides and hunters use to make their bears appear larger than they really are. Make sure the hide lays naturally flat, with no stretching.

In most areas, a black bear with a hide that squares 6 feet is considered a very good one. Hides squaring between $5^1/2$ and 6 feet are average. Anything under $5^1/2$ feet is a small bear. In areas that produce the largest bears, hides squaring more than 7 feet are seen on occasion. Bears with hides squaring more than 8 feet are rarely found. My largest bear to date was a bow kill from southeast Alaska in the spring of 2000. His hide squared

A hide that is rubbed, leaving bare spots, is the best reason of all not to take a specific black bear. Rubbed hides are most common in spring, after the bears have been out of the dens for a while.

an honest 7 feet 6 inches, and his skull measured 18⁸/16 inches.

Just as important as the size of the bear in determining trophy quality is the condition of the hair. Bears like to "rub" their hides on trees, stumps, rocks and other solid objects, as well as roll on their backs in sand, gravel, grass and dirt. They do this primarily in spring, when the weather warms and they try to shed some of that heavy winter hair. This leaves what are commonly referred to as "rub marks," which are really nothing more than patches of hair that have been rubbed off the hide, leaving bare or bald spots.

Rub marks can be quite large. I've seen many black bears with their entire rear end rubbed off. Large rubs also commonly appear on the legs,

belly, back, paws and forehead. Rub marks can also be subtle, sometimes nothing more than removal of the light guard hairs under the primary coat. It takes a trained eye to spot these kinds of rubs, which do not appear too bad at first, but which can result in a scruffy-looking hide once it comes back from the tannery.

It is important to carefully look over a bear for rub marks before deciding to take him. This is where your optics come into play. Use your optics to look the bruin over from head to toe, on both sides, before making a "yes" or "no" decision. If the bear is badly rubbed and one of your goals is to make a beautiful bear rug, or a shoulder or full-body mount, you'll be disappointed with a rubbed-up bear.

The World Records

The largest black bear listed in the Boone & Crockett book *Records of North American Big Game, 10th Edition* is a pick-up skull found in San Pete County, Utah, in 1975. It measures 14²/16 inches long by 8¹⁴/16 inches wide and scores 23¹⁰/16 points. The next largest is owned by the PA Game Commission and was taken in 1987 by an unlisted hunter. It measures 14⁸/16 inches long and 8¹⁵/16 inches wide and scores 23⁷/16 points. The minimum score to make the all-time Boone & Crockett Club record book is 21. Bears with skulls of this size are very rare indeed.

In the Pope & Young Club's fourth edition of *Bowhunting Records of North American Big Game*, the largest bear listed was taken in Kanawha County, West Virginia, in 1991. It measures 14¹/16 inches long, 8⁷/16 inches wide and scores 22⁸/16 points. The number two bear scores 22⁶/16 points and was taken at Gronlid, Saskatchewan, in 1992. It measures 13¹²/16 inches wide and 8¹⁰/16 inches long. The current world record listed on the Pope & Young Club's Web site was taken by Robert Shuttleworth in Mendocino County, California, in 1993 and scores 23³/16 points. The minimum score for entry in Pope & Young's all-time record book is 18.

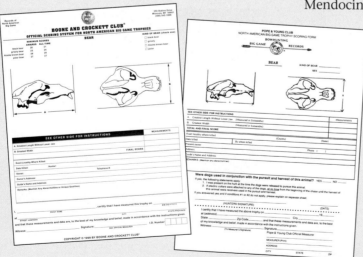

If you're wondering which gender of bears have the largest skulls, here's a graphic number. In the above-mentioned Pope & Young record book there are a total of 2,604 entries. Only 20 are sows.

FIELD-JUDGING BLACK BEARS

*I*n terms of trophy quality, field-judging bears is one of the most difficult tasks a hunter can face. How can you tell a big bear from a small one? After all, most big game hunters spend little time hunting bears, so they have limited, if any, experience.

Bears don't have easy-to-judge features like antlers. That's one of the reasons so many novice bear hunters shoot small bears. To them, any black bear looks big and that, coupled with a week of tough hunting and the threat of going home empty-handed, makes it so much easier to squeeze the trigger or release an arrow at a small bruin. To make matters worse, record-book entries are kept according to skull size, and it is flat impossible to look at a bear and say with any certainty, "Yep, he'll make the book."

To paraphrase the old carpenter's axiom, "Measure twice and cut once." Most of the time, black bear hunters have plenty of time before making the shot. You should have a fair chance to look the bear over, make sure it is a boar, evaluate the condition of the hide and relative size of the body, then say "yes" or "no."

Judging black bears is an art in and of itself. After a while, you'll see that big boars move differently than do sows and smaller boars. They just look tougher, bigger and stronger, walking with a barroom swagger that seems to say, "Hey dude! This is my neighborhood, so back off!" Unless provoked or startled, they move deliberately and are unafraid. Young boars, sows and sows with cubs do not have that swagger and tend to move more quickly.

Because a bear rug is the trophy most black

A trophy black bear consists of many things: a mature boar with a large skull, thick and luxurious hide, and big feet. With no antlers to look at, judging trophy size is difficult, especially when it comes to skull dimensions.

bear hunters covet, judging hide quality is paramount. This is where your high-quality optics earn their keep. You need to carefully look over the entire bear, from stem to stern, top to bottom, looking for the telltale rub marks that are the sign of an inferior hide. When rub marks are obvious, they stand out like a sore thumb. Big circular rub

Because a bear rug is the trophy most bears hunters covet, hide quality should be the paramount consideration when deciding whether or not a particular bear is a "shooter" or not. Look him over carefully before deciding!

patches on the hips, butt and back are the most common. Subtle rubs are harder to see. Sometimes just the delicate guard hairs on the belly line and legs are gone. These do not look too bad at first, but when you get the hide back from the tannery they can turn into blotches of hairless skin.

I've seen bears rubbed in the strangest places. One time in southeast Alaska, guide Jim Boyce and I watched a really big bear for a long time, wondering how in the heck he could have a perfect hide—except for the two circles of rubbed hide around both eyes. We called him the Raccoon.

Another time I was moving in on a very large spring bear feeding along a mountain ledge when, for no apparent reason, he stood up on his back legs and started rubbing his back on the sharp rocks. When he was finished he had a nearly hairless stripe down his back. I called him the Skunk.

In any event, it will pay to take your time in evaluating the quality of a bear's hide before deciding to take him home. And while there is no substitute for looking at lots of bears when it comes to judging how big they are, here are seven tips that will help you judge a bear's size, even on

A big boar appears to have small ears set on the side of his head. A record-class bear will have ears about 8 inches apart between the inside tips.

your first bear hunt.

1. Ears. Big bears appear to have small ears, because their heads are so large. A small bear will have ears that appear to be relatively large, sitting more on the very top of the head. The larger the bear, the more the ears appear to be on the side of the head. Also, a record-book class bear will have ears that are probably at least 8 inches apart between the inside tips.

2. Front feet. Measure the track of a front pad, add one, change inches to feet, and you have the approximate size the bear's hide will square. Thus, a $5^{1}/_{2}$-inch foot pad will carry a $6^{1}/_{2}$-foot boar, or male bear. Females rarely have front feet that exceed $4^{1}/_{2}$ inches in length. It must be stressed that this is just a rule of thumb, and there are exceptions to every rule. With bears, though, these exceptions are few and far between.

3. Body length. A female rarely exceeds $5^{1}/_{2}$ feet in length. Mature males are longer than that, with many trophy-class bears often more than 6 feet from nose to tail.

4. Snout. Big bears have what appears to be a short, squarish snout. We often refer to these snouts as a "stovepipe nose" set on a squarish head. Younger bears and females have what appears to be a longish, pointed snout set on a more sloping head.

5. Beer belly. A big male will have a large belly, even in spring, that will appear to almost brush the ground when he walks. This belly is much more defined in fall than in spring, when bears have yet to put on their winter weight. Younger bears have smaller, flatter bellies.

6. Height. A larger-than-average bear, when standing on all fours, will have a backline that reaches to, or above, the waist of an average-size man. If there is an upright 55-gallon drum at a bait site, it will have a pair of rings around it. If the bear's backline reaches above the second ring, it's a good bear.

7. Cubs. Big boars are loners, except during the rut, which occurs in late spring and early summer. Boars hate cubs. If there are cubs with a larger bear, it's a female. If the cubs scamper up a tree and the female begins to act nervous, get ready—a boar has possibly moved in.

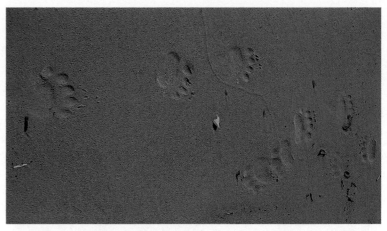

Measuring the width of a front pad track can give you a good idea of how big a bear is. Measure in inches, add one, and that number is approximately how big the hide will square in feet.

A mature boar has a short, squarish snout and, in the fall, a "beer belly" that will almost brush the ground.

When you spot a large bear with a very small companion, you can be sure it is a sow accompanied by one or more cubs. Mature boars are, by their very nature, loners.

Is It a Boar or Sow?

Because there are no antlers, and because most bear hunters actually see few bears in their lifetimes, telling the difference between a sow and boar when a single bear is spotted can be problematic. Mistakes are easily made, and sows are sometimes harvested by impatient hunters who could have waited for another bear to appear.

With that in mind, here are some tips on telling the sexes apart so that you can be more sure you are shooting at a boar bear.

1. Large boars look tougher, bigger and stronger than sows and young boars. Unless provoked or startled, boars move deliberately and unafraid, walking with a barroom swagger. Young boars, sows, and sows with cubs do not have that swagger and tend to move more quickly.

2. Boars have what appears to be a short, squarish snout, often referred to as a "stovepipe nose" set on a squarish head. Young boars and females have what appears to be a longish, pointed snout set on a more sloping head.

3. Though hard to see, in spring careful glassing can reveal the testicles of a boar between the hind legs. The penis is well hidden, but marked by a tuft of hair extending slightly forward of the rear legs. However, in fall the testicles have been drawn up into the abdomen and hidden by long fall hair.

4. Boars, generally speaking, appear long and lanky (though they often have a pot belly), while sows appear more squat and short. Sows rarely exceed $5\frac{1}{2}$ feet in length.

5. If two adult bears are seen together in spring, most likely the larger of the two is a boar, the other a sow.

6. In spring and summer, an adult accompanied by small bears is a sow with cubs. Boars are generally loners, except during the spring mating season.

Large boars simply look tougher, bigger and stronger than sows, and walk with a barroom swagger. They also have a short, squarish snout set on a squarish head.

Sows are smaller than mature boars, with more elongated, pointed snouts. Mature sows rarely exceed $5\frac{1}{2}$ feet in length.

WHERE THE BIGGEST BEARS LIVE

Okay, so you've decided to take the plunge and go in search of a real, honest-to-goodness trophy-class black bear. There are a million and one bear guides out there telling you they have 'em, all you have to do is show up and a monster will run out of the bush with its paws in the air in surrender.

Wisely, you're skeptical. You've heard all this before. The question is, where are your best chances for bagging a truly big black bear?

In Chapter 10, we'll discuss how to research good bear areas—those areas with the best trophy potential—and how to book a guided hunt, as well as present a black bear population forecast that can help with your planning.

But for now, the discussion is focused on specific areas where trophy-bear potential is great. As you read, keep in mind that anywhere black bears live, the odd whopper bruin could possibly emerge. The following areas have a proven track record in the production of monster black bears.

One secret to hunting a trophy-class animal of any species is that to have a real chance at harvesting a record-class animal, you have to hunt where they live. Since "book" bears do not live everywhere, you have to uncover where today's big bears are coming from.

Coastal Alaska and British Columbia, and their adjacent islands, are excellent places to hunt monster bears. California also holds some giants.

The upper Midwest—in portions of Minnesota, Wisconsin, Michigan and Manitoba—is home to some bruiser bruins.

Out West

Coastal Alaska and British Columbia, including many of the islands off Southeast Alaska, Vancouver and Queen Charlotte Islands, B.C., hold large numbers of big-bodied bears with relatively large skulls. Washington and Oregon have good bear numbers, but these bears tend to be a bit smaller than those found both farther north, in Canada and Alaska, and farther south, in California.

Surprisingly to some, California is one of the continent's true trophy black bear hot spots, with big bears found in both the northern and southern portions of the state. In the north, Glenn, Tehama and Trinity Counties are good bets. On the coast, Mendocino County is a proven producer. In southern California, Santa Barbara and Ventura Counties hold some absolute monster bears.

Farther inland, Arizona has produced some of the largest black bears ever taken, and continues to do so annually. Portions of Colorado, Idaho, New Mexico and Utah also produce many large bears each year. North of the border, in western Canada, Alberta and Saskatchewan kick out a disproportionate number of huge bears, as does Manitoba.

The Midwest

The upper Midwest—especially Wisconsin and Minnesota—produces many record-class bears with big bodies. In Wisconsin, Rusk, Washburn, Florence, Oconto, Iron, Bayfield, Polk and Douglas Counties are just a few of that state's better big bear areas. In the past five years, monster bears in Minnesota have come from Aitkin, Beltrami, Becker, Cass, Kanabec, Pine and Roseau Counties, among others. In Michigan, too, where huge bears thrive, Gogebic, Menominee and Wexford Counties have produced big bears, also in the past five years. And Ontario, Canada—one of the most popular bear hunting destinations—produces some enormous bears each year too.

The East & South

Farther East, Pennsylvania kicks out many monster bears per capita each year. Bedford, Bradford, Clarion, Clearfield, Clinton, Monroe, Potter and Tioga Counties are good places to look. In New York, the Adirondacks produce the most bears, and Delaware, Essex, Herkimer and Sullivan Counties produce some whoppers.

North Carolina is home to some big bears. Hyde, Craven, Bladen, Tyrrell and Onslow Counties are all good bets. There are some

Pennsylvania still produces some bomber bears, as does a strip through the Adirondacks. North Carolina and West Virginia likewise produce bears with big heads and huge bodies.

whopper bears in Virginia, too, with Rockingham, Alleghany, Bath and Augusta Counties being the state's four top overall bear producers. In West Virginia, Kanawha and Grant Counties hold some big bears.

THE FUTURE

With black bear populations expanding throughout the bear's range, look for some real whoppers to be taken in areas where bear hunting is an afterthought, or where no bear seasons have been held in generations.

Where might these big bears come from? New Jersey and Maryland are seeing more bear activity, and are considering allowing bear hunting again. Arkansas has expanded bear hunting opportunities in that state, thanks to a growing bruin population. And of course, the old standby trophy bear areas—led by the western Canadian provinces, the upper Midwest states, the western states of Alaska, California and Arizona, and the tobacco region that includes the Carolinas and Virginias, will continue to produce big bears in the foreseeable future.

With black bear populations expanding throughout their range, the future for hunting bears—and the harvest of some true monsters—remains bright. Stay atop current trends, and when you are ready to go out in search of a real trophy bear, you'll be able to select an area that is producing them now, not yesterday.

Chapter 9

MEAT & TROPHY CARE

My friends were suitably impressed. None of the 10 were hunters, yet when they walked into my home office and saw my collection of bear skulls displayed in an antique china cabinet, each of them closely surveyed the skulls. When I let my friends hold skulls and explained a little bit about each, they became much more interested. The beautiful bear rugs on my wall and the rack of tanned bear hides hanging nearby drew more comments. Soon I was well into a tale of hunting one particular big bear, an adventure that was more than a little bit hair-raising.

At dinner, we continued to talk about black bears. When supper was over, all commented on how delicious the meal was. When I told them the meat was taken from the big boar whose skull and hide they had been admiring a short time before, a bear I had shot that spring, there was a brief moment of silence and some perplexed looks. "You see," I said, "there is so much more to hunting bears than simply shooting one." That night, 10 non-hunters left my home as strong supporters of our sport. One woman even asked if I would take her along next spring.

Black bear hides, skulls and meat are precious to me. They come from an animal I admire greatly, and that I hunt hard every year, with great respect. However, poor field care is sure to result in meat that's inferior, hides with hair that slips and falls out, and skulls that crack and break in the years to come.

Making sure your own hard-earned bear is properly taken care of begins with meticulous field care: skinning your bear with care; keeping meat clean and cooling it down; preparing the skull. These are all skills you must learn. Thankfully it's not rocket science. The following pages will tell you what you need to know.

Skinning a bear isn't rocket science. You can do it—and do it well—with a few good tools, the right techniques and a little time and patience.

HOW TO SKIN A BEAR

Skinning a black bear for a rug, shoulder mount or life-size mount is not that complicated, though many folks make it seem so. The tough part is finishing the skinning process by removing the paws and head, which requires some dexterity and the right tools. My friends and I, who have skinned a truck bed full of bears, can peel the hide off an average black bear in about half an hour. The detail work of doing the paws and head adds some time. Here's what you need to do.

HAND PROTECTION

Before starting the skinning process, put on a pair of rubber gloves to protect yourself from infection. This is not a joke.

One time I was skinning an Alaska brown bear and deeply slashed the index finger of my left hand. It subsequently got very infected, to the point where it swelled up to twice the normal size, and I needed massive doses of antibiotics to stop the problem. The doctor told me that had I not gotten the right drugs soon enough, I might have lost the finger. (Today at temperatures of only 40 degrees or so that same finger turns white and throbs to beat the band.) Use either disposable surgical gloves, or my favorite, the heavy-duty gloves designed for doing the dishes.

Skinning a bear for a rug is simple: Roll him onto his back, make a cut down the center of the chest and the center of each leg to the pad on the paw, and go from there.

When you're skinning and butchering a black bear, wearing rubber gloves is extremely important to help you avoid infection.

READY, SET, GO!

Many times a bear will expire in a nasty place: a thick brush pile; in a cut, depression or canyon; a swamp or creek; or on the side of a steep mountain. While I have skinned several bears on steep mountainsides, it's neither fun nor easy.

The first step is always to move the bear to a flat spot that offers as much elbow room as you can create for yourself. Roll the bear on his back and spread the legs out the best you can. I carry an old beat-up space blanket in my pack, and use it as a makeshift ground cloth when skinning. This helps keep the meat as dust- and dirt-free as possible, given the circumstances.

It is a lot easier to skin a bear if there are two of

When skinning the bear, use one hand to keep a strong and steady pulling pressure on the hide, and skin with the other hand. Working with a partner makes the task much easier.

keep a strong, steady pulling pressure on the hide while skinning with the other. Your partner can help by lifting up the legs when needed and pulling on the hide.

It is best to skin one side of the bear first, including cutting off the feet, before starting on the other side. This helps keep the meat as clean as possible. The front feet can be removed easiest at the wrist joint, with the rear feet removed at the heel after cutting through the Achilles tendon. If I am not in a big hurry, I will skin the rear feet all the way to the toes, cutting the toes off and leaving them in the feet for removal later. I leave the front paws on at this time and work on them later at camp.

Once one side of the bear is skinned out, stretch out the loose hide and roll the carcass back on top of it. This will free up the other side for work. When this side has been skinned, work your way up to the neck, removing the head at the Atlas joint. It may take some searching for this large ball-and-socket joint, which is farther up the neck than many people realize, but once located it is easy to work through.

you—one to work the knife while the other holds the legs in the right position. Also, while some people gut their bears before skinning, I rarely do. The exception is if there is an easy way—ATV, for example—to haul the bear back to camp where it can be worked on in a clean and dry environment.

Once the bear is in position, prepare the bear for skinning by first making all the necessary cuts in the hide. Start at the base of the anus and cut around one side of the penis, between the testicles and straight up the middle to the throat.

Next, cut the legs from their approximate mid-point to the pads. Then skin around one side of the pad to the toes, following the inside of the pad.

Be sure to check state or province regulations before skinning the bear. Many places require that you leave evidence of sex attached to the bear until checked by an authorized agent of the government. That means leaving the testicles or vagina attached, so be sure to skin around them and not inadvertently cut them off. It is easy to do!

Once the basic cuts have been made, start skinning the bear. It works best if you use one hand to

Once the bear has been skinned, roll the hide up: Lay it hair-side down, fold the legs into the middle and the head down onto the chest, then roll the hide into a tight bundle. A good pack frame helps in packing it out.

Hunting Black Bears

It is necessary to remove the paws and skull from the hide carefully. The meticulous, fine work takes time and skill. If you don't have the expertise, get the hide to a taxidermist right away and let him or her do it for you.

BACK TO CAMP

Once the bear has been skinned, roll up the hide and prepare it for the trip back to camp. Lay it on its back, fold the four legs into the center, roll the head into the middle, then roll up the hide into a tight bundle. This will fit easily into your backpack or a large heavy-duty garbage sack or burlap bag for transport.

HEAD & PAWS

Skinning the head and paws is meticulous work that requires sharp blades and a deft touch. The toes must be skinned all the way to the end, with no fatty tissue left at the ends. When skinning the head, take time to cut the ears as close to the skull as possible, then carefully skin down into the ear cavity to remove the cartilage. Take great care when skinning along the ears and down to the lips and nose. The lips must be "split," that is, skinned back inside the mouth. Remember that any fatty tissue left can rot, which will result in

the hair slipping and falling out during the tanning process.

If you are not sure about how to correctly skin the paws and/or head, it is best to take the hide to your taxidermist and let him finish the job for you. Ask if you can watch, so next time you will be better prepared to try it yourself.

SALT OR FREEZE THE HIDE

Once the hide has been removed and the detail work is finished, it must be preserved to keep the hair from slipping. If I can get my hide to my taxidermist immediately, I do. However, this is usually not the case. If a freezer is available, I roll up the hide again as described earlier, stuff it into a heavy-duty plastic trash compactor bag, and freeze it solid. Hides will last almost indefinitely when frozen.

If I can't freeze the hide, I salt it. To salt a hide, lay it flat, flesh side up. Dump 5 to 10 pounds of fresh table salt in the middle and work it vigorously into the hide. Take care to work salt into

Once you've skinned the hide, you must either salt or freeze it before taking it to the taxidermist, to keep the hair from slipping. It takes about 20 pounds of fine table salt to do one good-sized black bear hide.

every nook and cranny of exposed skin, with extra emphasis around the face and toes. Once salted, roll up the hide and place it in a breathable sack—burlap or rice bags are excellent—and leave it overnight. The next morning, take it out, let the resulting liquid drain off, re-salt it and re-store it in your sack.

It takes 10 to 20 pounds of bulk table salt to salt a good-sized bear hide adequately.

Knives & Sharpeners

You need a sharp knife with which to skin a bear, period. Black bears have a fatty hide, and together with their longish hair and relatively thick hide, this combination can dull a knife quickly.

And you need to work to keep your knife sharp, as you go. A sharpening steel or small whetstone will help your skinning knife stay sharp during the entire job; pack one of these essential tools and have it with you.

You don't need a Bowie knife to do a bear either. My friend Mike Stitzel, a former Alaska bear guide, uses a custom-made skinner with a $3^{1}/_{2}$-inch blade for skinning; it is the best bear knife I have ever seen. It holds an edge almost forever, and the rounded blade makes it nearly impossible to accidentally poke a hole through the hide. I use a custom drop-point knife with a $4^{1}/_{2}$-inch blade, and it works like a champ. With it, I can do everything from skinning to removing the head and feet, as well as gutting the bear and boning out the meat.

For skinning out the paws and head, a slim-bladed, razor-sharp knife is your best choice. Many guides use surgical scalpels or X-ACTO knives with replaceable blades. When the blade gets dull, they throw it out and use a fresh one. One friend uses single-edged razor blades, like those used to cut carpet or cardboard. You need these slim, relatively narrow blades to work in tight quarters around the knuckles, up to the ends of the toes, and around the eyes, lips and ears.

Knives with nonskid handles made from natural bone or a synthetic material like Kraton will help you keep a good grip despite slippery blood and fat.

For basic bear-skinning work, a $3^{1}/_{2}$-inch to $4^{1}/_{2}$-inch blade is just right. You don't need a machete! Sharpness is the key.

THE SKULL

Bear skulls are cool. Properly taken care of, they make a most interesting addition to your den or trophy room. I have several skulls from black and grizzly bears I have taken, and I display them in an antique china cabinet in my office. It is always the first thing visitors comment on when they walk through the door.

To ensure that your bear skull will not deteriorate over time, you have to properly care for it from the get-go. Once you have the skull removed and fleshed, you can take it to your local taxidermist for care. He will either boil it for you, or send it to a "beetle man." These are folks who have beetles that can strip meat off a bone faster than

you can imagine. This costs a few more bucks, but results in a superior finished product, I believe. Also, boiling a skull may shrink it a little bit, which may be a problem if you want to enter it in the record book.

You can also boil and finish the skull yourself. Here's how to go about it.

1. Skin the head out. With a sharp, thin-blade knife, carefully skin the head out. Details on how to properly skin the head appear earlier in this chapter on page 135.

2. Remove the skull from the carcass. You can do this with your hunting knife. Cut the neck meat down to the Atlas joint in the neck at the base of

A bear skull is a cool trophy! Your local taxidermist can prepare it for you, or you can do it yourself. I send my skulls to a "beetle man," who uses insects to strip away all flesh and blood, leaving a superior finished product that will last for many years.

A proud hunter and his bear. The animal's skull will make a unique and attractive trophy. So will the beautiful skin; this particular bruiser's hide squared at a whopping 7¹/₂ feet!

the skull. By carefully working your knife between the ball-and-socket Atlas joint and carefully cutting and prying, the head will come right off.

3. Trim as much meat from the skull as you can with your hunting knife. Don't worry if the lower jaw comes off; it's supposed to. Take time to go up into the brain cavity with a small pointed object and dig out as much of the brain as you can.

4. In a well-ventilated area, i.e. outside, boil the skull in a large pot of water until all the meat is soft enough to come off easily. Make sure you keep the entire skull under water, or that part which is exposed to air will become discolored.

5. Using your fingers, a knife or a soft-bristle brush, remove all the meat.

6. In a clean glass (not metal) bowl or jar, submerge the skull in pure bleach. The bleach will soften first the cartilage, then the bone. The cartilage, found between the seams of the skull, will dissolve in a stream of bubbles. As soon as the bubbling stops, remove the skull and rinse it thoroughly in cold water to remove all traces of the bleach. This should take no more than a few min-

utes. Failure to remove the skull promptly will allow the bleach to attack the bone itself, damaging the skull.

7. Submerge the skull in a glass jar in a solution that is one part 3-percent hydrogen peroxide and one part water. Let the skull bleach for 6 to 8 hours.

8. Rinse thoroughly in cold water and air dry completely. Then wash the skull in gasoline or carbon tetrachloride, which will remove all the grease. Again, dry thoroughly.

9. Spread a light coat of Duco cement on the teeth to prevent them from cracking over time.

10. Spray the skull with a clear acrylic lacquer, like Krylon, which will keep outside dust, oils and other matter from staining or eating away at the bone.

Preparing your own bear skull is somewhat tedious, but also fun. If you have no experience in the matter, though, and are afraid something might go wrong and damage the skull, it is better to spend a few dollars and let a skilled taxidermist handle the job.

BUTCHERING & CARING FOR BEAR MEAT

Black bear meat is something you either like or you don't. Personally, I like it fine. Whole roasts and steaks are okay, but I really like what my local butcher does to the meat. He uses the bear meat I bring him each spring to make some fine Polish, breakfast and hot Italian sausages, and pepperoni sticks. They are superb eating.

One thing I have learned about bear meat is that you have to care for it properly in the field, or you will be greatly disappointed in the final product. The process begins the minute you decide to take the shot at the bear you want. Bears, like all game animals, just seem to end up tasting better if the first shot is placed squarely in the chest so that the animal dies quickly, with a minimum of running and thrashing about. Take your time and be sure of your shot before you squeeze the trigger or drop the bowstring. The animal deserves nothing less, and your meat will be the finest it can be.

AFTER THE SHOT

After you've made the shot and your bear is down for good, you have two choices: gut out the bear before skinning, or skin him out, and then butcher the meat.

Unless I am someplace where I can transport the bear using a vehicle—an ATV or pickup truck—and take it back to camp, I prefer to skin the bear first. If I can move the whole bear, I will

Once a big black bear is down, the work of skinning the bear and caring for the meat begins. Black bear meat is some of my favorite of all game meat, and I take meticulous care to make sure it is in prime condition when I get it to the butcher shop.

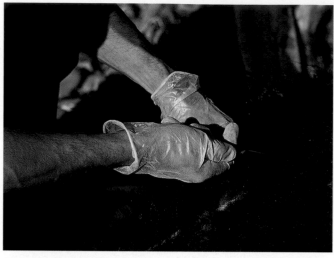

If you are near a road and easy transportation, field dress the bear by removing the digestive system, heart and lungs, then transport the carcass to camp or town for final skinning and butchering. Don't forget to wear your rubber gloves!

plastic trash compactor bags in my hunting pack. Before I start skinning my bear, I lift up the half I'll be working on first and slide the space blanket (or small tarp) under the animal, then let it back down on top of the plastic. This creates about as clean a butchering environment as you can have in the field.

Okay, you've got one side of the bear skinned up to the neck, and the paws are off. Have your hunting partner hold each rear leg up, and remove the ham by cutting up near the pelvis, using your knife to cut through the connective tissue and meat holding the ball-and-socket joint together. It will come off easily. Take the ham and place it in one of those heavy-duty plastic trash compactor bags, where it will stay clean.

Next, remove the front shoulder. With your partner holding the front leg up, cut into the armpit behind the scapula. The whole shoulder will come off easily. Put the meat in the garbage bag.

The backstrap comes off next. This long, narrow muscle is located against the backbone, from the hips to the front shoulder. Cut down along the backbone, pulling the strap away as you cut. Bone it off from the top of the ribs, and you'll have it.

Now roll the bear over. First, stretch his hide out away from the body, so that when you roll him over he lays back down on it. Now skin out the other side and repeat the butchering process. When finished, you'll have four quarters and a pair of backstraps. Now remove the head as described in the previous chapter, using your knife to cut through the Atlas joint. If you want some neck meat for burgers, now's the time to get it. Simply bone it off the neck.

Voilà! You've now taken the choicest cuts off your bear, without dealing with the blood-and-guts mess that occurs when you gut it out first. I field

gut it and get the meat cooling during transportation to camp.

Skinning the bear first has two benefits. One, it is always easier to peel off the hide while the bear is still warm. And two, by skinning the bear I am not worried about creating a bloody mess that will get all over the hide and the edible meat.

Earlier in this chapter, we said the best thing to do is move your bear to a flat spot where it can lay level, and you can stand or kneel without worrying about falling off a cliff before getting to work. You've done that and you're ready to go. What's next?

DO HALF THE BEAR FIRST

When skinning the bear, we also previously discussed the advantages of doing one half of the bear first, then rolling him over and doing the other half. This is as opposed to doing both hams first, then working forward. The reason is simple—this way you can keep both the hide and the meat off the ground and away from as much dirt and debris as possible. This is your goal when field-dressing your bear—keeping the meat as clean and dirt-free as you can.

To this end, I always carry an old space blanket and several large, heavy-duty

The dotted lines show the primary cuts for skinning a bear.

dress virtually all my big game animals this way.

If you want the ribs—which have little meat on a black bear—use a small pack saw to cut them off, taking care to avoid puncturing the organs of the digestive tract. If you take the ribs, you can also work up under the backbone with your knife and bone off the tenderloins. These are the choice cuts of any animal, and on a black bear they are fairly small, but they're definitely worth retrieving.

BONE IT OUT?

Because I have virtually all my bear meat turned into sausages, I bone it out and trim it up before taking it to my butcher. That saves me money, because most butchers charge by the pound, and the extra weight of the heavy bones would add to the cost. If butchers have to take the bone out, they'll often ding you for that too.

A large black bear can yield upwards of 100 pounds of boned-out meat, hide and skull. If I am backpack hunting on my own—something I commonly do in the mountains near home—and shoot a bear, I need to reduce the weight as much as I can to make packing everything back to camp or to my truck possible for my middle-aged body. That means boning the meat out.

In my pack I carry a boning knife, which is similar to a filet knife except that the blade is a bit stiffer and only $4^1/_2$ inches long. This knife is ideal for working around the bones and taking meat off in big chunks. Boning meat is a straightforward process. You simply work the meat until there are no bones left.

On the hams, make a circle, cut all the way around the ankle, then slice the meat to the femur and cut along the femur all the way up to the ball joint. Then work the knife carefully around the femur, and before you know it you'll have a classic boned-out ham.

You do not have to bone out the meat, of course. Some butchers prefer getting the meat on the bone, so be sure to ask yours what they would rather work with before you head off hunting.

COOL IT DOWN, CLEAN IT UP

Cooling the meat is paramount. Bear meat can go bad in a hurry, especially in hot spring weather, so make sure it gets cooled quickly.

Those plastic garbage bags we used to keep it

You need only a few simple tools to skin and butcher a bear with professionalism. I always have what I need in my hunting pack. You may not need the saw, but it could help the task along.

clean in the field are the worst possible meat storage bags, because they trap heat and induce spoilage. The exception is if the meat is put on ice in an ice chest, in which case the plastic bags are great because they keep the meat dry as it rests on the ice.

Once back to camp, if there is no ice around, it is time to get the meat out of the plastic and hang it to cool down rapidly. I use heavy-duty cheesecloth-type game bags (those from Alaska Game Bag, phone 931/525-3626, fax 931/520-0726 are the best I have ever used) and hang them in the shade where a cool breeze can hit them. The cheesecloth bags help keep dirt, dust and egg-laying flies and insects off the meat. Before hanging the meat, take the time to wash off all the blood and as much of the dirt and junk that inevitably gets on it in the field.

Before taking your meat to the butcher, take some time to trim it up. Remove as much of the field junk—little sticks, twigs, leaves and dirt—as you can. Trim away all the fat. Bear fat will give your meat a poor taste. Always remember that even the finished products of the best butcher and sausage maker in the world are only as good as the meat he has to work with. Give him the prime stuff, well-cared-for in the field, then trimmed and washed up, and he'll give you some of the finest eating meat you'll ever taste.

COOKING TIPS

lack bear meat is delicious and full of protein. I particularly like the meat from spring bears that have been munching on fresh green shoots and grasses. The meat is a dark red color and generally layered (not marbled) on the outside with a greasy fat that is best removed before butchering, freezing and preparing. The fat can go rancid easily and it can give the meat an overly greasy feel and taste.

Like pork, bear meat has been known to carry the parasite *Trichinella spiralis*, which can cause the disease trichinosis. While this parasite is rare, to help ensure that it is not passed along to the consumer, it is important to cook the bear meat long enough to kill the parasite should it be present. With fresh pork, the recommended cooking

time and temperature is 375°F for 20 to 25 minutes per pound of meat. For cuts weighing 3 pounds or more, the recommended cooking time is double that. A temperature of 137°F will kill the parasite, but the recommended internal roasting temperature is 170°F, just to be on the safe side.

If you don't have a meat thermometer, a good rule of thumb is to cook the meat thoroughly throughout, until there is no trace of pink flesh or fluid, especially in the joints and close to the bone. Freezing will not kill the parasite in uncooked meat. Also, cooking in a microwave oven may not kill the *Trichinella* parasite, and is therefore not recommended.

Bear meat tends to cook "dry," meaning that unless you are careful in your preparations, it can

Crockpot Roast with Cranberries.

end up being tough and stringy. One way to avoid that is to cook it "wet"; that is, use sauces, soups and broths to help keep it moist during cooking. A bit of water to steam the meat also helps, as does cooking large cuts like roasts and hams in a Dutch oven or slow cooker.

Bear meat is delicious as is. However, you may try marinating it before cooking to add flavor and to tenderize it. The same marinades that work well with pork roasts, ribs and large cuts of beef, like chuck roasts, work well with bear meat. Bear meat also makes great burritos and is excellent in casserole-type dishes like enchiladas, chili and stews.

My favorite thing to do with bear meat, though, is take it to my local butcher and have him turn it into a wide variety of the sausage products mentioned. I also like bear meat made into a variety of meat sticks. Lightly barbecuing Polish sausage after slathering it with your favorite barbecue sauce is superb. Hot Italian sausages in a hoagie-type roll make unbeatable sandwiches. The list goes on.

Here are a few select recipes to try with your next black bear.

CROCKPOT ROAST WITH CRANBERRIES*

1 (10$^1/_2$-ounce) can double
   strength beef broth
$^1/_2$ can water
$^1/_4$ tsp. ground cinnamon
2-3 tsp. cream-style
   prepared horseradish
1 (16-oz.) can whole berry
   cranberry sauce
1 bear roast (3-4 pounds)
Salt and pepper to taste

Place broth, water, cinnamon, horseradish and cranberry sauce in a medium saucepan; bring to a boil while stirring constantly. Place roast in crockpot. Pour sauce over roast and cook on low 6-8 hours or until roast is tender. Pass juice with roast.

* Recipe adapted from the NAHC cookbook *Wild Bounty* by Jim and Ann Casada.

BEAR ROAST

1 medium bear roast
2 medium potatoes, cubed
4 medium carrots, diced
$^1/_2$ yellow onion, diced
2 T. crushed garlic
1 T. Worcestershire sauce

Boil roast on stove for 1 hour. Drain, cool and trim excess fat. Place in slow cooker, cover with water. Add vegetables and garlic. Cook on low for 4 hours. Add Worcestershire sauce. Continue cooking on low for 4 more hours.

BBQ BEAR CHOPS

4 bear chops, 1 to
   1$^1/_2$ inches thick
4 T. butter or margarine
1 12-oz. can beer

BARBECUE SAUCE
1 tsp. lemon juice
1 cup ketchup
$^1/_4$ cup brown sugar
2 T. horseradish
Salt and pepper to taste
Minced garlic
Minced onion to taste

Trim excess fat from chops. Brown on both sides in skillet using butter or margarine. Drain off excess butter. Place chops in skillet, turn heat up to high, add enough beer to cover $^1/_2$ inch up sides of skillet, cover with lid or aluminum foil and steam for 10 to 15 minutes. In the meantime, mix lemon juice, ketchup, brown sugar, horseradish, salt, pepper, garlic and onion, and heat to boiling. Remove chops from skillet, baste both sides with barbecue sauce and place on aluminum foil. Bake in preheated 350°F oven for 20 to 30 minutes. Serve with extra barbecue sauce if desired.

Chapter 10

HOW TO BOOK A GUIDED HUNT

*I*t's a common yet sad story. A group of four hunting buddies from the same whitetail camp decided that it was time they did some black bear hunting. At a sport show, they met a central Canadian outfitter who ran bait hunts out of his fishing lodge in spring. The price was right—$900 per person per week—and the boys jumped on it.

When they got to camp, they quickly realized you get what you pay for. There were a slug of other hunters in camp, and not enough guides or vehicles to take them all hunting at reasonable hours. When one of the rigs broke down, hunting stopped for a day while the camp staff repaired it. The baits were poorly maintained, the stands were old, rickety, set without any real cover, and had obviously been hunted to death. Out of the 20 hunters in camp that week, five shot bears, all of them two-year-old peewees. Two of our four hunters never saw hair.

A high percentage of black bears are hunted with guides and outfitters, both in the United States and across Canada. Dissatisfied bear hunting clients are common. It seems like just about anyone and everyone who does some sort of outdoor recreation in bear country is also a "bear guide."

If a guided bear hunt is your dream, it is imperative that before you open your wallet, you carefully analyze both prospective outfitters and the areas in which they hunt. That means becoming a researcher, trying to ferret out good bear areas just as if you were going to hunt there on your own.

While I hunt bears hard on my own each year, I have taken several guided bear hunts in the past. Some of my most memorable—and successful—bear hunts have been with guides. If you've never been bear hunting before, going guided is an excellent way to increase your odds for success.

Want to up your odds at not getting ripped off? Then keep reading ...

RESEARCHING TO FIND THE BEST BEAR AREAS

*T*he key to any serious big game hunter's consistent success can be summarized in three simple words: *planning* and *hard work*. It's easy to get so fired up about the hunt itself that we sometimes forget that without careful planning and research, the hunt can be doomed from day one. Without pre-hunt research, any success in the mountains or big woods will be as much the result of blind luck as skill.

Whether I will be hunting with a guide or on my own, I want to be hunting in the best area I can for whatever species I am seeking. I'm not willing to leave my success to chance, and neither should you. That's why you need to become a researcher. After all, before you can shoot a bear,

you first have to find one. With limited hunting time, you need to maximize time spent afield, hunting where the bears are, not where they are not. Research is the key.

Here's a step-by-step process on how to research new hunting areas.

STEP ONE: CREATE FILES

In my home office I have several files that help me plan my hunts. Into my "black bear" file each year go all sorts of things—magazine articles, maps, harvest statistics, state game statistics, notes from books, and so on. For each state I am considering hunting, I also have separate files that con-

Big bears like this don't walk into your lap. Good research will start you on your way, though.

Creating files to store all your research materials will make your search for the right bear guide a systematic, successful task.

tain the coming year's hunting regulations and license and tag application procedures. These items help me choose new areas I may want to hunt, based on information that tells me what's hot and what's not.

Keeping everything in a file folder makes it easier for me to keep track of the several different hunting trips I'm planning for the coming year, and hunts I'm dreaming about for future years.

Step Two: Contact Game Departments

Contact the game departments of the states you're considering and get the coming year's regulations. Bear seasons vary widely by state, as do application procedures, due dates and costs. And these days, it seems as if states are changing the way they do things almost annually. The regulation booklets spell out these changes. Ask the department if they have current harvest statistics available. Many states do. These numbers will help paint a broad portrait of hunter success and distribution, harvest by area and trophy quality.

Step Three: Maps, Maps, Maps

Once you've narrowed your choice of a hunting area to a general location, it's time for maps. The United States Forest Service and the Bureau of Land Management each have public land maps within specific states that help you locate boundaries, roads, water sources, timbered ridges, campgrounds, trails and trail heads. I like general state maps too, which show major roads and towns. Together, all these maps give me a good overview of the area I might want to hunt.

Later in the process it will be time for United States Geological Survey topographic maps. These maps show too small an area for initial planning, but are essential for the final planning and hunt execution phases of your trip, so hold off on buy-

ing them just yet. I use the larger maps to help me define the general area I want to hunt, then topo maps to show me the details. Topo maps are more valuable when hunting on your own, but I like them for guided hunts too.

I can't overemphasize the importance of maps, both in planning and during the actual hunt itself. Without them, I feel as blind as the proverbial bat.

Step Four: Talk & Write

The final stage of the planning process is talking with people. Maps can give you a general overview of the area, but people can fill in the blanks and give you an accurate, up-to-the-minute picture of what the area is really like.

"Up-to-date" is the key phrase here. While maps are invaluable, you'll rarely find one that's up-to-date. New roads, towns, subdivisions, trails, logging operations, fires, and so on, may not be shown on maps, but local people may know about them and help you fill in the blanks.

Try to talk with state game department biologists whenever possible. When I talk to these folks, I try to work my way down, not up, the

Talking with people—biologists, guides and outfitters, and hunters on a guide's reference list—are all part of setting up a successful bear hunt.

departmental flow chart. I don't want the man in charge of half the state—I want the local biologist for a specific forest or drainage or region I'm considering hunting.

The same holds true for game wardens, forest service personnel and so on. These people work right in the area, and can fill me in on current conditions and bear population numbers. These people may be hard to locate, and it may take several phone calls to actually hook up with them once you've found out who they are, but it is time and money well spent.

Whenever possible, I also try to talk with local hunters, taxidermists and any other contacts I can think of. I try to ask as many people as I can the same questions, then "balance" their answers in my mind.

STEP FIVE: USGS TOPOGRAPHIC MAPS

About the time I start calling, writing and e-mailing people, I like to buy topographic maps of the areas I'm pretty sure I'm going to hunt. Topo maps help me pinpoint specific creeks, drainages, ridges and so on where my research tells me the game should be when I arrive. Topo maps also allow me to ask the people I'm calling very specific questions about the area. I coat my topos with a clear waterproof sealer so that I can write notes on them during my research, detailing information I pick up talking with people.

Topo maps help me narrow things down from general information to specific terrain features, areas that may receive lots of pressure from other hunters, the best ways to access the hunting grounds, and so on. When I'm done with my research, my topo maps closely resemble those used in military operations.

Research. I know it's more like school than hunting, and it sure isn't as much fun as putting your binoculars on a big black bear's shiny coat

Topographic maps used in conjunction with the telephone help me pinpoint potential bear hot spots before I ever leave home.

rippling in the evening sun. But it's all part of the chess game, a way to tip the odds for success in your favor, and to keep the fire burning during the off-season. You get to talk hunting with other folks and maybe make some new friends.

Researching areas to hunt trophy-sized black bears is a two-step process. First, you have to find an area that holds the kind of bears you're looking for. Then you have to hunt them in such a manner that you maximize your odds of seeing them during legal shooting hours.

Finding an area that holds trophy bears today—not yesterday—is the most difficult task faced by hunters. By systematically approaching the problem and breaking the search process into pieces, it becomes easier to put the puzzle together. As mentioned, I call the process "shrinking your focus."

By that I mean you have to shrink the area you'll be hunting to a manageable, realistic piece of ground that can be hunted thoroughly.

Step one is selecting a state to hunt. Then, by a process of elimination, choose a single mountain range or national forest in that state. Next, select a small area of that often vast mountain range, forest or swamp, from which more specific river or creek drainages are chosen. The final step is deciding at what elevation and in what kind of cover those areas will be hunted.

Trophy bear hunters don't approach this process haphazardly. Most are looking for a new trophy bear hot spot all year 'round. They have discovered that the key to finding such a spot is information.

To that end, I begin the area search process by reading. I read magazine articles and books and watch videos. I contact game departments and ask for data on bears—harvest data, boar/sow ratios, population data, and so on. I also study the Boone & Crockett and Pope & Young record books. These sources of information get me started both by telling me historically where big bears have come from (meaning bears in these areas have the genetics to grow large bodies and skulls), and by giving me hard data on current population levels.

Next, I start talking to anybody and everybody who might give me a lead.

Potential Trophy Hot Spots

Biologists, foresters, taxidermists, other hunters, ranchers, cowboys, sheepherders, backpackers, hunting guides and outfitters, and others like them who are intimately familiar with a given area, just might give me a lead.

Naturally, I take everything with a grain of salt when talking with these people. Knowing that they might mislead me a bit, I try to confirm a promising tidbit of information by asking others about it in a roundabout fashion. Only after I confirm it do I begin to get excited.

I always ask about food and water as well as local range conditions. Has there been a drought? If so, has it affected bear numbers? What do bears eat in this area, both in spring and fall? What are their preferred food sources—those foods they will go out of their way to eat above all others? If I don't know what those plants look like, I go to the library and get a book that shows me, so I can identify them once I'm in the woods. Have there been any large fires? Timber cuttings? New roads?

It's important to remember that, while an area that has

When researching potential hot bear hunting areas in a quest for a bruin like this, I always try to shrink down the size of a large area into a smaller, huntable location consisting of a single drainage, lake area, swamp or river course.

produced record-class bears in the past has the potential to do so at any given time, "hot" areas for big bears can change seasonally. That's why research and information are so important. Nothing is more frustrating than heading for a hunting area expecting the best, only to find that the hot spot you or someone you know hunted last year is now a golf course or ski resort or has been ravaged by fire.

Because most of us do not live in good black bear country, we have to do our research by telephone and/or on the Internet. We don't have the luxury of physically scouting all year around, so we depend on the information we gather as our primary source of locating new areas to hunt. The more meticulous you are in doing so, the better your chances of hanging a giant bear rug on your wall.

ALL GUIDED HUNTS ARE NOT CREATED EQUAL

Since the early 1980s, I've been on more than my share of guided hunts. This has included hunts all across North America, as well as internationally. Fortunately, most of these adventures have been great. However, some have not. The question is, how can you ensure that the black bear hunt you booked will be your dream come true, and not a twisted nightmare?

One word: research. You have to research potential outfitters the same way you research hot hunting areas. This takes time and effort on your part. In the long run it will pay big dividends.

One way to find a quality bear outfitter is to meet and speak with several at one of the many sport shows around the country.

Every year I meet excited hunters who book with the first outfitter they meet, believing the hype and hoopla and plunking their money down without comparison shopping. Sometimes these trips turn out great. Often they do not.

Quite honestly, there are a number of outfitters out there who are slicker than snake oil salesmen, fudging the facts so they can more easily tap your bank account. These guys show you lots of pictures of satisfied clients, giving the impression that such success is routine. They forget to tell you the last time they killed a really big bear, disco was in and gas cost 50 cents a gallon.

First off, you must have realistic expectations about a guided hunting trip. Remember that booking a guided trip does not guarantee you'll kill a bear, let alone a monster bruin. What it should guarantee is that you'll be provided with solid food, a comfortable camp, a guide who knows his stuff and is willing to work hard, and the opportunity to hunt an area where you have a reasonably good chance of finding the type of animal you desire.

Before contacting prospective outfitters, there are some questions you need to honestly answer about why you want to go on a guided hunt. These questions apply to all guided hunting, not just trips for black bears. Here are those questions:

What animal do you really want to hunt? Sounds basic, but many people do not target a single species as their priority. If hunting a big bear is your goal, with a mountain goat or elk secondary but nice if one happens along, you want to choose an outfitter in an area with lots of bears and a solid track record of success, not one in an area with lots of goats or elk but just a few bears.

Is taking an animal more important than the quality of the experience? If so, you're setting yourself up for disappointment. Even the best guides and outfitters have weeks where the animals and/or weather don't cooperate. If an outfitter historically has gotten 75 percent of his clients an animal, you just may be in the 25 percent who return empty-handed. Somebody has to be. There are no guarantees of success in fair-chase hunting. The best you can do is play the odds—and there are places where the chances for success are better than others.

Are you willing to do what it takes to prepare for the hunt? You can't expect to take a good bear on a tough spot-and-stalk mountain hunt if you are not in good enough physical condition to make it up and down the mountain. Will you take time before the hunt to practice with your weapon, so that you are able to take advantage of the one good but fleeting opportunity that presents itself during a week's hunt? The inability to walk, and poor shooting skills, are the two most common complaints outfitters have about clients.

What type of camp and hunting style will you be happy with? Is camping in a small backpack tent okay with you, or do you prefer the comfort of a lodge with a soft bed? Would you prefer to hunt while floating a river, or hiking among the peaks? Do you mind riding horses? Does tree-stand hunting over bait bore you, or is this what you prefer? How many other hunters will be too many for you to share camp with? Be honest with yourself, or you'll end up being miserable.

Always ask prospective outfitters about what type of camps, food and amenities they have, so you can match your likes with a camp that provides what you are looking for.

Only after being honest with yourself is it time to seek out individual outfitters. There are several ways to do this. I've met lots of top outfitters at some of the major hunting and fishing shows held around the country. Sport shows are great places to interact personally with outfitters and get on-the-spot answers to your questions. Advertisements in the back of magazines like *North American Hunter* are another source. Using a booking agent who represents several different outfitters is one way to help shorten the research process. Word of mouth from friends who have hunted with a particular outfit before is perhaps your best source of information.

Finally, give yourself enough time to plan your trip, locate a suitable outfitter and set aside vacation time. Most top outfitters book the majority of their hunts a year or more in advance. Rushing the process is a good way to make a mistake that could turn your dream into endless grief.

10 QUESTIONS YOU MUST ASK

Before any money changes hands, ask prospective outfitters the following 10 questions.

1. What animals do you hunt? What are the species with top trophy potential in your area? If you want a big black bear, with an average elk as your secondary goal, but the area has only a few bears and lots of elk, you're probably hunting in the wrong place.

2. How many actual hunting days will I have? On a 10-day hunt, you may have one day's travel time each way in and out of the hunting area, cutting the actual hunt time to eight days. If you're stranded in base camp for extra days

On a guided hunt, you are not the expert or leader. Remember this before you book and when you're formulating your expectations.

A guided hunt can get you a big bear and net you a wonderful experience ... if you do your homework.

because the outfitter is having problems, will he allow you to extend your hunt to compensate for missed days afield that were not your fault? The outfitter can't control the weather, but he should be in control of his equipment, staff and scheduling.

3. How many hunters and support people will there be in camp? To avoid overcrowding, you want to know how many other hunters will be in camp. Also ask if your guide doubles as the cook, horse wrangler and wood cutter. Generally, but not always, it's better if the guide does nothing except take you hunting.

4. How many hunters per guide? Do you have a guide all to yourself, or will you be sharing him with another client? Though it costs more, on spot-and-stalk hunts it's almost always more productive to hunt one-on-one. If you get to camp and your one-on-one hunt is suddenly a two-on-one affair, immediately solve the problem with the outfitter. In larger bait-hunting camps, this ratio is not as critical.

5. How long have you been hunting in your area? I prefer to hunt with people who have been outfitting an area for at least three seasons, and therefore know the area and local game movements well.

6. How long have your guides worked for you? The outfitter will rarely take you hunting himself. You want a guide with experience hunting both the area and the species you're targeting. Don't settle for a first-year guide as your primary guide.

7. Are your guides experienced bowhunters themselves? Have they successfully guided bowhunters before? It is very important for bowhunters to have a guide who understands the unique requirements of hunting with archery tackle. There are few non-bowhunters who make good bowhunting guides.

8. What percentage of your clients are repeat customers? If the outfitter was lousy and there was no game in the area, he'd probably not have many repeat clients. Repeat business is a good indicator of a reputable outfit.

9. What does the hunt package cost? You'll be quoted a hunt cost of, say, $2,500 for a guided black bear spot-and-stalk hunt. Now ask about any "hidden" costs like licenses and tags (rarely included in the hunt price), trophy and meat care, tips and gratuities, additional charges if you take another animal and so on. Is there a "trophy fee" for actually harvesting an animal, or for taking an animal that scores exceptionally well by record book standards? These "extras" can add hundreds of dollars to a hunt's base price. No one likes to be surprised.

10. Do you have references I can contact? Ask not only for a list of successful clients, but also clients who did not get game on their hunt. Ask for references within the last three years. Spend a few bucks and call them all, and ask lots of questions regarding all aspects of the hunt. If an outfitter won't provide references, avoid him.

The best bear camps offer reasonably good odds for success and provide good accommodations, good food and extensive knowledge of local bear habits.

Different Strokes for Different Folks

O nce you begin researching bear guides, you'll quickly discover that there are several different types of black bear hunts out there. It is important to decide what will make you happy, and to read between the lines when talking with prospective outfitters.

For example, there are many different bait hunting operations spread across Canada. But just because they all use bait does not make them equal. Some are fishing lodges set in good bear country that bait bears as an afterthought, a little secondary income before fishing season is in full swing. Some bring in way too many clients for the number of bears they have, and their success rates on mature bears reflect this. Some operations have harvested too many bears for too long, which results in low bear numbers in the specific areas they hunt, and a noticeable lack of boars older than three years. These camps continue to get hunters because they charge very little money.

On the flip side, there are bait hunt operations that carefully monitor both the number of bears they take each year, and the size of the bears they take. They have a high success rate on large boars because they work hard at it. They may charge more money, but generally speaking, you get what you pay for.

The same is true for both spot-and-stalk guides and houndsmen.

What this means is that you have to decide exactly what kind of experience you want to have before passing along your hard-earned Jacksons to a bear outfitter. Tell him exactly the type of hunt you want, the kind of bear you're looking for and what kind of hunting style and camp will make you happy. Be sure to call and check references. After all, you're going hunting to please yourself, not the outfitter.

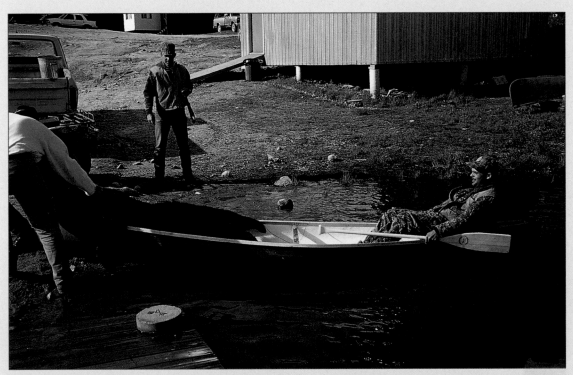

What kind of bear hunting experience do you want? Is the chance at a monster bear more important than seeing lots of bears? Would you rather hunt from a canoe or a treestand? Discuss your wants and needs with potential outfitters before any money changes hands; do all you can to make sure you'll be happy once the hunt is nothing but a memory.

Black Bear Hunting at a Glance

In all U.S. states and Canadian provinces that currently permit black bear hunting—at the time of this writing, that's a total of 27 states and 11 provinces—prospects are at least good, if not excellent, for a successful hunt. In some states and provinces, no spring hunting is allowed. Actual season dates will vary from year to year, so be sure to check with the state or province you are thinking about hunting to get specific season dates as well as any other restrictions that may apply. The population estimates below are just that—estimates. Use them as a guide, but don't take them as gospel. Biologists will tell you that they themselves are not exactly sure how many bears live in their state or province. That's bears for you: secretive, elusive, hard to really know. Also, note that regulations on spring and fall hunting, as well as bait and hound hunting, will evolve.

Bottom line? Bear hunting prospects will change with time. Use the information at right to stay in contact with state and provincial game agencies.

Where are the most bears today? Counting black bears is an inexact science at best, but the states and provinces with the highest bear estimates will probably remain at the top for years to come.

Black Bear States and Provinces

State or Province	Estimated Black Bear Population	Fish and Game Department Phone Number	Fish and Game Department Web Site
UNITED STATES			
Alaska	150,000	907-465-4190	www.state.ak.us/adfg
Arizona	3,000	602-942-3000	www.azgfd.com
Arkansas	3,500	800-364-4263	www.agfc.com
California	25,000	916-227-2271	www.dfg.ca.gov
Colorado	12,000	303-297-1192	www.dnr.state.co.us/wildlife
Georgia	2,300	770-918-6416	www.dnr.state.ga.us
Idaho	25,000	208-334-3700	www.state.id.us/fishgame
Maine	23,000	207-287-8000	www.state.me.us/ifw
Massachusetts	2,000	617-727-3151	www.state.ma.us/dfwele
Michigan	15,000	517-373-1263	www.dnr.state.mi.us/wildlife/
Minnesota	28,000	651-296-6157	www.dnr.state.mn.us
Montana	not available	406-444-2535	www.fwp.state.mt.us
New Hampshire	5,000	603-271-3422	www.wildlife.state.nh.us
New Mexico	6,000	505-827-7911	www.gmfsh.state.nm.us
New York	5,000	518-457-3521	www.dec.state.ny.us
North Carolina	9,500	919-733-7291	www.state.nc.us/wildlife/
Oregon	27,500	503-872-5268	www.dfw.state.or.us/
Pennsylvania	9,000	717-787-4250	www.pgc.state.pa.us
South Carolina	500	803-734-3888	www.dnr.state.sc.us
Tennessee	2,000	615-781-6585	www.state.tn.us/twra.html
Utah	1,200	801-538-4700, 877-592-5169	www.nr.state.ut.us/dwr.htm
Vermont	3,500	802-241-3700	www.anr.state.vt.us/fw/fwhome
Virginia	4,500	804-367-1000	www.dgif.state.va.us
Washington	35,000	360-902-2200	www.wa.gov/wdfw/
West Virginia	9,000	304-558-2758	www.dnr.state.wv.us
Wisconsin	13,000	608-266-2621	www.dnr.state.wi.us
Wyoming	not available	307-777-4600	gf.state.wy.us
CANADA			
Alberta	37,000	780-427-5185	www.env.gov.ab.ca/
British Columbia	150,000	250-387-9422	ww.env.gov.bc.ca
Manitoba	30,000	800-214-6497, 204-945-6784	www.gov.mb.ca/natres
New Brunswick	15,000	506-453-2440	www.gov.nb.ca/
Newfoundland	8,000	709-729-2630	www.public.gov.nf.ca.tourism
Northwest Territories	10,000	867-977-2350	N/A
Nova Scotia	8,000	902-424-5935	www.gov.ns.ca/natr/
Nunavut*	not available	not available	not available
Ontario	100,000	705-755-2000	www.mnr.gov.on.ca
Quebec	60,000	418-643-6662	N/A
Saskatchewan	30,000	306-787-2314	www.serm.gov.sk.ca
Yukon Territory	10,000	867-667-5221	www.gov.yk.ca/

*As of this printing, Nunavut does not yet have a structured wildlife agency. Up-to-date information is available in the NAHC Hunting Resource Directory available through the NAHC Member Services Department.

Chapter 11

ARE BLACK BEARS DANGEROUS?

D id you grow up with teddy bears at home? Did you watch Yogi Bear cartoons? Did Smokey Bear come to your grade school and talk about how to prevent forest fires? Have you come across TV shows that depict black bears as cute, playful, fun-loving pranksters?

After learning about a black bear breaking into cars parked in a national forest campground or invading an uncovered trash dumpster near town, many people think, "How cute. What lovable pranksters these bears are!" Increasingly, though, we hear about black bears attacking campers or hikers. At least twice in a recent year, unprovoked black bears have killed people. Stories of bear attacks are easy to find, especially on the Internet.

Although black bears are generally shy, leave-me-alone animals, they are big, powerful, speedy omnivores that can—and sometimes do—attack and kill people. As more people move into bear country, both to recreate and to live, bear encounters will increase. Unless these people learn to live cleanly with the bears, bear encounters will increase.

As a bear hunter, you should always treat a black bear with the respect it deserves. Never let your guard down or get careless when in bear country. Always keep a clean camp. Know what to do if confronted by a bear that won't go away. Learn what to do, and be prepared to defend yourself, should a black bear decide that you are a snack.

A wise man once said that preparation is everything. The chances that you'll ever have a bear problem are remote. But by being prepared to handle the worst, and by respecting the power and speed of a sometimes dangerous animal that has been known to attack and eat people, you can hunt in bear country with confidence.

Here's what you need to know …

BLACK BEAR ATTACKS

The screaming headline said it all: "Woman Killed by Bear in Tennessee." Associated Press reporter Duncan Mansfield wrote about Glenda Ann Bradley, age 50, who became the first person killed by a black bear in a federal park or reserve in the southeastern United States. She was mauled in the Great Smoky Mountains National Park while hiking and waiting for her ex-husband, who was her hiking companion but not with her at the time. "This was simply an unprovoked attack,"

said Phil Francis, the park's acting superintendent. The bear was a 111-pound adult female with a yearling; both were later shot and killed by rangers.

Rangers had tagged this same adult bear in 1998 and had placed an orphaned cub with her. Park officials said the animal wasn't known as a problem bear.

That wasn't the end of fatal black bear attacks that year. In July, a 24-year-old female athlete, Mary-Beth Miller of Yellowknife, Northwest Territories, Canada, was killed by a black bear while running on a training course in a heavily wooded area just north of Quebec City, Quebec, police reports said. Miller was a member of Biathlon Canada, the national biathlon association.

These are just the most recent examples of fatalities involving black bears.

The year 1992 was especially bad for black bear attacks. In June, Krystal Gadd, age 9, was sleeping in her grandparents' camper in Utah when she was awakened by something smashing through the window. Suddenly, something clamped around her head and dragged her, sleeping bag and all, out the window. Sleeping in another vehicle was her grandfather, George Gadd, who shined his flashlight at the sound—and right into the eyes of a large black bear.

When Gadd shouted at the bear, the bear ran off, dragging the girl in her sleeping bag along. Fortunately, the bear came to a barbed wire fence, which snagged the bag. Gadd grabbed the girl and yelled for her to run back to the camper.

Black bears are big, powerful, speedy omnivores that will sometimes attack people with the intent to kill and eat them. They are animals to be respected at all times by hunters, hikers and others who live and recreate in bear country.

But when she did, the bear charged the pair repeatedly, only to be confused and repulsed each time by the flashlight beam.

A woman living near Glennallen, Alaska, was not so fortunate. A rogue black bear chased her and a male companion up on top of their remote cabin. With no firearm available for protection, the man jumped down, got into a boat and sped across a lake for help. That's when the bear climbed up on the roof, knocked the woman off and killed her. It was feeding on her body when help arrived.

Want more? A 52-year-old Colorado man was bowhunting elk in the Buffalo Peaks Wilderness Area. He had shot a cow elk, and a 250-pound sow bear tried to take it from him. The hunter, who shot the cow and left it overnight before coming back the next morning to pack it out, found that a large portion of the meat had been eaten by a bear the night before. Believing the bear was no longer around, he skinned the remaining meat and began to hang it in a tree. That's when the bear, which had been sleeping nearby, charged.

The man climbed 10 feet up the tree, but the bear followed. The hunter repeatedly kicked the bear in the nose, which backed it down. Still, it made four charges up the tree before Colorado Division of Wildlife Conservation Officer Randy Hancock, who had volunteered to help the man pack out his meat, arrived on the scene about two hours later. As he got closer, the man in the tree yelled a warning to Hancock when the bear made another charge up the tree. Hancock told the treed man to hang on, he was going back to his truck for a rifle. He returned and killed the bear, an animal that obviously was not going to give up "her" meat.

More than once, I have had a black bear try to climb up the tree in which I was sitting over a bear bait. For that reason, where legal when bowhunting over baits, I also always carry a large-caliber firearm just in case.

AGGRESSIVE BLACK BEARS

Black bear/human conflicts are on the rise all across the bear's range. To understand why, all you have to do is look at the combination of a growing black bear population coupled with the increasing encroachment of people into prime bear habitat. Add to that the fact that most people today are urbanites with a limited knowledge of the harsh realities of nature and who were raised to believe that black bears are playful, cuddly and cute, and you have a formula for trouble.

Way back when, someone invented something called the "teddy bear," one of the most popular toys of all time. Baby Boomers—those city folk nearing retirement age who are building most of the vacation cabins and homes in what was formerly wild country—bring a Disneyesque image of wildlife with them. Heck, they grew up with "Smokey Bear," the United States Forest Service's world-famous firefighting mascot. Two of their most popular cartoon characters were a pair of lovable bears named Yogi and Boo-Boo. How can people not think that bears just want to be playful and friendly?

Dr. Stephen Herrero of the University of Calgary in Alberta, Canada, is perhaps the world's foremost authority on black bear attacks. He has documented several dozen cases over the past 50 years of black bears aggressively attacking and eating humans. Many of these attacks were unprovoked.

Curiosity & Hunger

Most bear/human conflicts revolve around two things—the bruin's seemingly insatiable appetite, and its inquisitive nature.

Black bears can, and do, eat just about anything they can digest—and some things they can't.

For example, one thing bears just can't seem to walk past without biting are plastic gas cans. Whether it is the gasoline or the plastic that draws them, no one is sure, but you can bet their curious nature will get them into unattended plastic gas cans every time.

Bears that break into cabins and vehicles will bite, chew, roll, push and shove anything and everything they can find that might be or hold something edible.

And break into vehicles they will. In California's Yosemite National Park in just one recent year, black bears broke into 1,100 vehicles looking for an easy meal. Damage was estimated at $634,000.

Bears have learned that people leave food in their vehicles. It makes no difference that the doors are locked—bears are not ordinary thieves. They know food in a car makes a very easy meal; park officials know that some individual bears learn to break into specific makes and models of vehicles, and can do so faster than any experienced car thief. Favorite methods of entry include smashing out windows and ripping off doors.

Leaving food carelessly around a campsite in bear country is like sending a black bear an engraved invitation to lunch.

One of the most common mistakes people make while camping in bear country is to cook and/or eat in their tent. The first thing a black bear will do when it comes to camp is seek out food odors, then rip up anything and everything where the food smell is. If that's your tent and sleeping bag, kiss them goodbye—even if you're in it. It is better to cook and eat under a separate shelter with lots of ventilation, like a large tarp. Try to cook and eat downwind from your sleeping area.

Conflicts in campgrounds are increasing across the country. One example occurred in the Angeles National Forest near Los Angeles. There, a young bear mauled 8-year-old Juan Valle, who had been attending UCLA's UniCamp for underprivileged Los Angeles County children. Valle was sleeping when the incident occurred, with the bear leaving three deep gashes on the boy's head and face. Federal officers later tracked and killed the bear.

While there are no statistics to back this up, many people believe that human/black bear conflicts increase when the bear's natural food supply is less than adequate for an area's bear population. Thus, in years of poor berry crops or drought, or after fires have burned up the bears' natural food sources, bears must search in other places for enough to eat. Often this leads them to unprotected dumpsters, garbage dumps, campgrounds, cabins and vehicles parked at trailheads.

Bears are driven by hunger and curiosity. In parks and campgrounds, bears have learned that people leave food in cars, and the animals know how to break into those cars to get it.

The fact is that there are more bear/human conflicts these days than ever before. If a deer, elk or moose meets a hiker or camper, the animal's inclination is to leave the area. But bears are different. They have large home ranges, are reasonably territorial and often get very aggressive when protecting a food source or their young.

As humans continue to encroach on bears and the wilderness in which they live, conflicts are inevitable. Push the bears far enough, and they are more willing to lash out to protect themselves. And while black bears would just as soon mind their own business, they are only animals. Tempt them with food and they will come get it. It's up to us to make sure we do not encourage them in this regard.

Avoiding Conflicts

By nature, black bears are shy creatures that just want to be left alone. However, carelessness will draw them to you, creating trouble. To minimize potential problems, experts recommend the following steps:

Residential Prevention
1. Take down, clean and put away bird feeders by mid-April. Clean up spilled seed at feeder stations.
2. Keep garbage in closed "bear-proof" containers inside your garage or storage shed, not on the curb. Put garbage out on the morning of collection, not the night before.
3. Do not place meat or sweet foods in a compost pile.
4. Do not leave pet food or dishes outside after your pet has eaten.
5. Clean and store outdoor grills after use.
6. Do not intentionally feed bears in or near your yard for viewing.

Camping Prevention
1. Maintain a clean campsite.
2. Put food scraps and drippings in a closed container, not the campfire.
3. Do not cook or eat in your tent.
4. Keep food and cooking gear separate from your sleeping area.
5. Hang food at least 10 feet off the ground and five feet out on a limb that will not support a bear. If available, store food in bear-proof containers.
6. Do not feed bears.

Agricultural Prevention
1. Use electric fencing around beehives and livestock.
2. Bury or incinerate livestock carcasses.
3. Alternate row crops to provide less bear cover.
4. Monitor field crops in late summer to detect damage.

The best way to store food in bear country is high off the ground, strung between two branches so bears cannot climb the tree and get it.

If you sense that a black bear is aggressive, be on the alert for a potential attack. If he comes for you, he'll want to eat you. Don't play dead as you would with a grizzly; instead, stand your ground or fight for your life!

IF YOU'RE ATTACKED

The odds are you're never going to be attacked by a black bear. Regardless of what you do in the woods—hunting, fishing, hiking or camping—unless you're having a really bad day you should never have to worry about bear trouble. Lightning maybe. A bad fall, possibly. Hypothermia, it can happen. But a bear attack? That's an occurrence with such poor odds that no self-respecting bookie would take the bet.

And yet, as we have seen, every year people do get attacked by black bears. Rarely are these people hunters. If you start tracking wounded bears into thick cover, however, all bets are off. Bad things can quickly happen then. Like having good insurance, it just makes sense to be prepared for the worst when hunting in bear country.

So what do you do if you're attacked by a black bear?

FIGHT OR PLAY DEAD?

In grizzly country, the rule of thumb is that if you are attacked by a griz you should not offer any resistance. Instead you should drop to the ground, curl into a fetal position with your legs drawn up to protect your midsection and groin, and clasp your hands behind your head to protect your head and neck. Draw your chin down to your chest and tuck your head in to protect the throat and face. Let the bear work you over if it wants to, but do not scream or thrash. If the attack stops, lie there for a while, in case the bear is still close by waiting for you to move.

The reasoning behind this theory is that grizzlies rarely attack humans to eat them. Instead, it is usually a territorial thing, with sows protecting cubs or bears guarding a food source. The same is true if you happen to startle a grizzly in thick brush.

With black bears, however, the consensus seems to be that you'd best fight for your life, because when a black bear attacks, it will try to eat you.

Black bear expert Dr. Stephen Herrero's advice is plain. "Black bears are not grizzlies," he says. "Playing dead isn't the thing to do. Running away is foolish, as this can trigger the bear's chase instinct and besides, you have no chance of out-running a bear that wants to catch you. Climbing trees doesn't usually work, because any tree that will support you will probably support a bear. It is better to stand your ground, make yourself look as large as you can, and yell loudly. Try to intimidate the bear into thinking you are tougher than he is, and he may back off."

It is important never to let a black bear think you are easy pickings. If he has had an easy meal in your camp, a nearby dump or another food source near you, your mere presence may not be enough to stop him from coming back and trying to eat there again. If you're in the way, the bear may think you are a threat to that easy meal, and decide to fight you for it.

BEAR ENCOUNTERS

Most bears that are encountered have not yet seen, heard or smelled your human presence. Once they do, they'll usually leave. However, if a bear refuses to leave, stay calm and talk to it, quietly and calmly at first, but yell if you have to. If there are other people nearby, attract their attention. Groups of people can be intimidating to a bear when an individual is not.

At the same time, look for a stout limb that can be used as a club. Back away from the bear slowly, but keep facing it. Avoid direct eye contact, as bears may perceive this as a threat. Look around for other bears, especially cubs. If you see them, try to keep from getting between the sow and the cubs. A sow's maternal instinct is to protect her cubs at all costs, and if she perceives you as a threat to them, the odds are good she'll try to get rid of the problem—you.

Be aware of the bear's body language. If a bear lays its ears back and its hair is standing up, especially along the neck and backline, it is one mad bear. If it pops its teeth, snaps its jaws or swats the air or adjacent vegetation, it is signaling you to back off. A bear that stands on its hind legs or puts its nose up in the air is not necessarily threatening you but is probably trying to get a better view or smell of you as it tries to identify what you are.

Try to always face the bear. If it tries to circle

you, turn with it. Do not run. If you have a day-pack, fishing gear, or anything else that might distract the bear or smells like food, you might leave it between you and the bear as you slowly back off while still facing the bruin. The bear might stop to sniff or swat these items about while you make a controlled retreat. If you find a good club, swinging it through the air while hollering may slow the bear down. If it gets too close and you feel that you need to hit it, the end of the nose is a delicate place and will hurt him.

Of course the best defense against bear attacks is to avoid them by not placing yourself in a precarious position to begin with. You have to use your judgment in how to act and what to do, of course, as every situation is unique. If you have a firearm or pepper spray, using it can save you (see sidebar). These should be the last resort, however.

If you encounter black bears unexpectedly, try always to face the bear; if it tries to circle you, turn with it. Look for a stout limb that you can use as a club. If the bear attacks, experts say your best chance is to fight for your life rather than play dead as you would with a grizzly.

Hunting Black Bears

The Lowdown on Bear Repellant

There are two common types of bear repellants: so-called pepper spray, and a large-caliber firearm.

Pepper sprays were first introduced a couple decades ago with Counter Assault, the inception of Dr. Charles Jonkel, then working for the Montana-based Border Grizzly Project. He developed this product as a means of deterring grizzly bear attacks by other than the use of deadly force.

In subsequent years, several different brands of pepper sprays have been introduced to the marketplace. The active ingredient in these sprays, oleoresin capsicum, is derived from hot chile peppers. The liquid sprays out of the can in a concentrated mist like a shotgun blast. The pepper, or capsicum, irritates the upper respiratory system and mucous membranes of the eyes and sinus. Once hit in the face with a blast of the spray, a bear can think only of finding relief, and will break off the attack. These are the same basic pepper spray products used by police departments and other people for personal protection.

Pepper sprays have proven reasonably effective in deterring grizzly attacks.

Pepper spray has not been proven 100 percent effective in repelling black bears. If you choose to carry pepper spray, do so on a belt holster within easy reach.

However, a 1999 study done in Alaska by United States Geologic Survey researcher Tom Smith showed that while pepper sprays can be effective in turning a charging grizzly or brown bear, their smell and residue can actually attract them. (It is recommended that you do not test-fire a pepper spray can around camp for that reason.) These sprays have been less effective in turning attacking black bears. Though pepper spray has worked, there are cases when bears have ignored it and pressed the attack.

If you choose to carry pepper spray, do so in a belt holster that permits quick, easy access. Experts also recommend at least a 4-ounce can, as these contain the highest concentration of capsicum and are capable of spraying a sustained blast for more than a minute.

The other alternative, of course, is a firearm. Where legal, this is my choice for hunting—even when I'm bowhunting. I have made a habit of carrying my short-barreled .375 H&H Mag. into my treestand when hunting over baits, just in case. I know if I have a problem, this will solve it.

William R. Meehan and John F. Thilenius of the United States Forest Service in Alaska conducted a study to determine which cartridges were most effective as "bear stoppers." They were concerned primarily with large-bodied brown bears, but their findings can be applied to all bears. They concluded that the best overall bear-stopping cartridges were, in order, the .458 Win. Mag., the .460 Wthby Mag., the .375 H&H Mag. and the .338 Win. Mag. They also found a .30-06 with 220-grain bullets was a good choice for standard-caliber rifles, and that a 12 gauge shotgun loaded with rifled slugs was also a good choice.

Chapter 12

IS BLACK BEAR HUNTING DOOMED?

uring a recent spring, I was sitting near the crest of a tall mountain in coastal Alaska. The view was spectacular, the air pure and the feeling I had inside was one of uninhibited freedom. I had climbed 2,000 vertical feet through thigh-deep snow and thick brush to reach a small grassy meadow in which a good black bear had been feeding earlier.

I got to thinking about how special that day was, and how lucky I was to be able to hunt black bears. And then a feeling of sadness crept in as I thought about the threats that black bear hunting faces in the near future.

Today there are more black bears across the continent than in any time in recent history. Thanks to solid management programs and lots of protected areas where bears can live peacefully and reproduce, bear numbers continue to grow.

And yet, many people continue to chip away against bear hunting. Bait and hound hunting have recently been eliminated in some places, and challenges loom large on the horizon for those types of hunting in areas where they remain legal. Anti-hunters are targeting all forms of bear hunting.

Despite all this, as I climbed down the mountain my spirits soared. With a lot of education and hard work on the part of the hunting fraternity, the future of black bears—and black bear hunting—is bright. As long as bear populations remain strong, through knowledge and diligence we should be able to continue our sport. It is my hope that your children, and their children, will experience the same feeling I had on that mountain while stalking one of North America's truly wonderful game animals, *Ursus Americanus*.

THE FUTURE OF BLACK BEAR HUNTING

Black bear hunting is addictive. I happily admit to being one who spends far too much time each year planning and executing bear hunts. The reasons have nothing to do with success. If the truth be known, for every bear I've taken, I've spent at least two or three weeks savoring the chase. That's just the way do-it-yourself bear hunting goes.

I've hunted them about every way you can. In the spring, I run bait stations near my home. While my friends are all out chasing turkeys, I'm scouting out new bait sites, or spending the days spot-and-stalk hunting bears on the steep, vibrant green mountainsides.

I've battled bad weather and rough seas boating along the coast of Alaska, spotting bears as they

Black bears are magnificent. Hunting them is an adventure. We need to work together to preserve both bears and bear hunting.

gorge themselves on fresh grasses and old, smelly carrion. In the fall, I always spend at least a week hunting bears, usually spotting and stalking them, but not always. I've followed the sound of the hounds pursuing bears up, down and all around some of the steepest, thickest terrain imaginable.

After all that, one thing I can definitely say about hunting black bears is that it is certainly not boring.

BEAR POPULATIONS GROWING

The good news is that black bear populations are growing all across the animal's range. While counting bears is anything but an exact science, estimates put the number at slightly fewer than one million. That's an increase from the estimated 550,000 bears—370,000 of them in Canada—of 1977.

And black bears are showing up in places where there were never any, or very many. Maryland, which never reported any bears, now counts several hundred. New York, New Jersey and Florida, among other states, have reported measurable

Research is helping us understand bears better and, in turn, manage them better.

bear population increases. One recent April, wandering bears forced the closure of a 2,500-acre swath of the popular Cohutta Wilderness Area, part of the Chattahoochee National Forest in the mountains of northwestern Georgia. California's bear numbers have skyrocketed in the past two decades to the point where there are now bears occasionally seen in downtown areas along the foothills.

One graphic example of a black bear increase is Ohio—where they are currently protected as an endangered species. Here bears are moving in from neighboring West Virginia and Pennsylvania, reviving a presence not seen in 200 years, according to state wildlife officers.

By the mid-1800s, bears virtually had vanished from Ohio, thanks to hunting and the loss of forest habitat. No one knows exactly how many bears are currently living in Ohio. The number of sightings has increased annually in the years since the wildlife division began formally tracking bears. In fact, say wildlife officers, if the bear population in Ohio continues to grow at the current estimated rate, there could be enough bears to hunt in 20 years.

Another good example can be found in Massachusetts, where biologists from the Department of Fisheries and Wildlife began trapping and radio collaring bears to help study a rapid increase of the bear population in the western part of the state. At the beginning of the effort, the state's bear population was estimated at about 500. That number has increased to nearly 2,000. Hunters harvest an average of 70 bears annually, which is not enough to stop the population from continuing to expand rapidly, biologists say.

There are several reasons for the growth of

In biological terms, the future of black bear hunting is bright across the board. Bear populations are growing throughout their range, and bears are showing up in new areas every year.

black bear numbers across the continent. These include: improved habitat; a dramatic shift in attitudes toward bears, from that of fur bearer and varmint, endangered by unlimited hunting, to that of big game animal, protected by tightly restricted hunting seasons and controlled harvests; and the establishment of protected park lands, especially in the eastern United States (Great Smoky Mountain National Park in Tennessee and North Carolina, Adirondack State Park in New York and Florida's Everglades National Park, among others) that have given bears protected places where they can regenerate.

The bad news is that black bear hunting is under serious attack, and not because sport hunting poses any biological threat to bear populations across the board. It is because the sport has become the focus of anti-hunting groups large and small that perceive it to be a weak link to be exploited first in their overall scheme of outlawing all forms of hunting.

BEAR HUNTING UNDER ATTACK

Despite the increase in black bear numbers, bear hunting continues to be under heavy attack

Improved habitat, tightly controlled hunting seasons, protection from harvesting sows with cubs: All have aided in the resurgence of black bear populations.

With bears venturing into areas where they have not been found in recent years, the chances for new bear hunting seasons are good.

from the radical anti-hunting faction. It is this threat, and not a lack of black bears or a wholesale degradation of black bear habitat, that threatens the future of North American black bear hunting more than anything else. In addition, in this day of exploding growth in human population, the habitat factor must constantly be watched.

As is their style, the anti's chip away at bear hunting rather than attack it head-on. Their current tactic is to try to outlaw spring hunting outright, or if that doesn't work, then eliminate hunting bears over baits. This they call "unethical" and "murder," and claim it results in the killing of too many sows with cubs. In reality, baiting black bears is very hard work. In the flat, heavily forested areas of the North, it is the only practical way to harvest bears. And baiting allows hunters to look over bears closely before deciding to pull the trigger, in effect making it the best way there is to harvest a high percentage of mature boars, which game managers prefer.

To eliminate baiting, the anti's have resorted to statewide ballot initiatives backed by massive advertising campaigns, as well as state and federal lawsuits.

For example, in 1992, Colorado voted 70 percent to 30 percent to stop spring black bear hunting, and all bait and hound hunting. In 1994,

Oregon voters banned bait and hound hunting for bears. In 1996, the Fund for Animals and five other local groups filed suit in federal court against both the United States Forest Service and the state of Wyoming to make bear baiting illegal on all national forest lands, contending that for the federal government to make baiting the responsibility of individual states violated the National Environmental Policy Act and the Endangered Species Act. Fortunately, that suit was dismissed in federal court in October, 1997. Did that run the anti's out of the game? Nope. Fund for Animals spokesperson Andrea Lococo of Jackson, Wyoming, said that in the wake of this decision the Fund was "exploring its options" concerning the bear baiting issue.

The latest blow against black bear hunting occurred in Ontario, Canada, where roughly 70 percent of all black bear hunters are traveling Americans who pump some $40 million into the economy. Thanks to the efforts of a well-funded publicity campaign and hard politicking, the province outlawed spring bear hunting. And the

Winnipeg, Manitoba, Humane Society urged the provincial government to end spring bear hunting because, a WHS spokeswoman said, "cubs aren't yet old enough to fend for themselves and can die if left without a mother." This despite the fact that shooting sows with cubs is against Manitoba law!

THE INITIATIVE PROCESS

It is the ballot initiative process—an important part of our form of government—which now allows uneducated voters to override the game management decisions made by trained, dedicated biologists, dictating how wildlife shall, or shall not, be managed. When these campaigns are conducted by the anti-hunting groups that are inevitably behind them, the bears are portrayed as warm, soft, cute, cuddly and intelligent, the friend of man. This is not an image that lends itself to support of regulated sport hunting of black bears as part of a game management plan. Also, surveys have shown that many people genuinely believe that black bears are an endangered species.

Despite healthy bear populations, black bear hunting is under constant attack from anti-hunting groups who see this "poster child" animal as a good way to get into the minds, and the wallets, of uninformed people coast to coast.

Is Black Bear Hunting Doomed?

The Colorado initiative was an eye-opener. There, both rural and urban residents voted about equally to support the measure. Also, both hunters and non-hunters willingly voted to stop certain forms of bear hunting—baiting and the use of hounds. Can you believe that 14 percent of the amendment's supporters were active hunters, and another 12 percent said they had previously hunted? As an aside, a survey of bear hunters in Michigan in 1992 showed that 33 percent of dog hunters opposed baiting, while 33 percent of baiters opposed hound hunting.

It is appalling that, in this day and age of hunting under attack, some hunters choose to judge and oppose other law-abiding hunters.

THE CAPITULATION APPROACH

If we are to defeat the anti-hunters, sport hunters need to stand strong in their defense of all hunting, and not just black bear hunting. Do not let anti's divide us over hunting method. Just because you don't hunt bears over bait or with hounds, or only hunt them in the fall and not the spring, stand up for the rights of others to whom these methods and seasons are important. Choosing whether to hunt bears over bait or with hounds—historically, both traditional and viable forms of bear hunting—should be left to each individual. The initiative approach takes that option away from the individual.

The capitulation approach theory says that if hunters draw a line on what is or is not an acceptable form of hunting, then get rid of those objectionable forms of hunting, that the non-hunting public will support all other forms of hunting.

Yet history shows that regardless of the concessions hunters make to the anti-hunting groups today, anti's will be back tomorrow to attack those forms that remain. D.R. Shubert, head of investigations for the Fund for Animals—a notorious anti-hunting group—once said in an interview, "Our objective is to eliminate all forms of sport hunting. We try to take on those hunts and meth-

Anti-hunting groups continue to use the ballot initiative process as a means of ending black bear hunting in areas where they think they can be successful. They start by trying to eliminate baiting or hound hunting, but their true goal is to stop all hunting.

Hunting Black Bears

As long there is wild country across the continent and urban sprawl doesn't encroach too deeply into our forests and mountains, black bear populations will remain strong, and hunting them will be a legal and thrilling activity. As hunters, our job is to fight to preserve that wild land, and to make hunting all-inclusive for men, women and children, so that the tradition continues.

ods that are most objectionable. As we whittle it down, we convert hunters to anti-hunters." All hunters, regardless of the methods they choose, must respect the methods others choose, as long as they are within the law.

WHAT DOES THE FUTURE HOLD?

Black bear hunting is indeed one of North America's most exciting and challenging hunts. Those who become students of bear habits and haunts, who are willing to spend lots of days scouting and then hunting while perhaps not seeing much, but are then prepared to make the right moves and take a good shot when they do see a bear, are the ones who can truly call themselves bear hunters. They'll also be better woodsmen for their efforts.

With bear numbers slowly increasing across much of North America, some states that have not held a black bear season in many years could seriously consider permitting the harvest of a few bears by special permit in the not-too-distant future. That interest is high in such hunting

opportunity is evidenced by the competition for the limited draw permits issued in upper Midwestern states like Wisconsin and Minnesota.

As long as there is wild country across North America, as long as urban sprawl does not encroach too deeply upon our forests and mountains, as long as we have both large tracts of parklands and wilderness areas where black bears can reproduce and live in solitude, the future of our bear populations is bright.

With those states that continue to offer black bear hunting closely controlling the harvest as they learn more and more about their bears, we can be assured that sport hunting will never be the reason that bear numbers have declined. And as long as we do not let the radical anti-hunting faction take away our bear hunting opportunities one piece at a time, there is no reason to think that your children's children will not be able to experience the thrill of hunting one of our continent's truly special big game animals—the black bear.

INDEX